Leisure, Family and Lifestyle

Leisure, Family and Lifestyle

Unemployed Young People

Francis Lobo

RAWAT PUBLICATIONS

Jaipur and New Delhi

ISBN 81-7033-751-8
© Author, 2002

Published by
Prem Rawat for *Rawat Publications*
Satyam Apts., Sector 3, Jain Temple Road, Jawahar Nagar, Jaipur - 4 (India)
Phone: 0141 651748 / 657006 Fax: 0141 651748
E-mail : info@rawatbooks.com
Website: www.rawatbooks.com

Delhi Office
G-4, 4832/24, Ansari Road, Daryaganj, New Delhi 110 002
Phone: 011-3263290

Typeset by Rawat Computers, Jaipur
Printed at Chaman Enterprises, New Delhi

Dedicated to:
The numerous young unemployed people who
struggle against all odds to be reemployed.

Contents

Acknowledgements

I wish to thank Healthway, the Western Australian Health Promotion Foundation, for funding a project that is a serious community concern. Implementation of the recommendations will be of benefit for the health and wellbeing of young people who are unemployed and who do not use public sport and leisure resources.

I offer special thanks to all the participants in various phases of the study. They included over 100 young males and females. Giving their time to be interviewed is much appreciated. More importantly, their suggestions to make life more tolerable have been helpful in my understanding of the deprivations they encounter.

I am also grateful to the nine Recreation Officers of local authorities. Their perceptions of problems for young people have been invaluable. Suggestions to facilitate greater inclusion have been seriously noted.

Stanley Parker, my co-author of the previous *Later Career and Unemployment* book, also gave valuable advice at the final preparatory and editorial stage of the present project.

Finally, thank you to Mike Tomlinson, my research assistant who spent many hour of interviewing on my behalf. Despite several disappointments when participants did not show up at set times and days, he managed to gather substantial data form which meaningful inferences could be made.

Francis Lobo

List of Tables

1

Introduction

Unemployment and its consequences is one of the worst social problems facing the world today. Increasing globalisation, making it easier to export jobs, is only adding to the problem. The biggest battalions in the reserve army of the unemployed are young people and those in 'late career'. This study focuses on the former. Although Western Australia experiences a lower unemployment rate than the rest of the nation, it is still considered unacceptably high. Public discussion of unemployment has focused on economic effects but the health impact has largely been ignored. Effects of unemployment on lifestyle in the leisure domain have been researched by Lobo (1994) but that study was confined to mature-aged persons. Very little has been done on young adults. This study focuses on the deprivations of unemployment and how it affects the health and lifestyles of young people.

Objectives

The objectives of the project are:
1. To assess the impact of unemployment on the leisure activities of young adults;

2. To ameliorate the impact of job loss through the provision of sport and recreation; and
3. To enhance commitment to healthy lifestyles of young unemployed adults through sport and recreation programs.

Unemployment, Leisure and Health

The term leisure is used to mean any activity (or inactivity) undertaken freely for the enjoyment it yields (Glyptis, 1989). Sport and recreation are regarded as leisure activities in this study. The literature reveals that unemployment affects individuals, their health and leisure in unpleasant ways. Little attention has been paid by public agencies to reduce the impact of job loss through sport and recreation programs, though community institutions have given assistance for basic necessities arising from poverty caused by joblessness. This project examines the possibilities of delivering programs to unemployed young people so as to restore, at least partially, their health and quality of life enjoyed during paid employment.

Unemployment and the Individual

The effects of unemployment on the individual have been studied from various perspectives. Human consequences resulting from unemployment have profound effects on one's self-concept (Kelvin & Jarrett, 1985). Unemployment causes stigma, a deeply discrediting attribute (Goffman, 1968) and causes the individuals who suffer it to see themselves as social inferiors (Kelvin & Jarrett, 1985). Hayes and Nutman (1981) have shown how an individual's personal identity developed, managed and affirmed in employment changes to the status of welfare dependent in unemployment.

Unemployment and Health

Cross-sectional and longitudinal studies on health effects confirm that unemployed people generally experience higher levels of depression, anxiety and general distress, together with lower self-esteem and confidence. Fryer and Warr (1984) report a slowing down of cognitive and problem-solving activity in a study of unskilled and semi-skilled unemployed men aged 16 to 64. Thirty-seven percent of men indicated that they were taking longer to do things they previously did, and 30 percent that they were getting "rusty" at things they used to do well.

Studies by Warr and Jackson (1984) and Payne, Warr and Hartley (1984) reveal that between 20 and 30 percent of unemployed men reported deterioration since job loss. Mental health changes were typically described in terms of increased anxiety, depression, insomnia, irritability, lack of confidence, listlessness and general nervousness. Unemployed people also describe a worsening of psychosomatic conditions such as dermatitis, eczema, headaches, high blood pressure and ulcers.

In their longitudinal studies on families, Fagin and Little (1984) conclude that health problems play an important part in adjustment to unemployed life. A depressive picture is characterised by feelings of sadness, hopelessness and self-blame, worthlessness and loss of self-esteem, inability to communicate feelings resulting in withdrawal and isolation, lack of energy, feeling constantly tired, loss or gain in weight, suicidal tendency, irritability, sometimes accompanied by impulsive and occasionally violent outbursts, abuse of alcohol and cigarettes and insomnia. The foregoing findings give rise to the following question:

What is the impact of unemployment on young adults?

Unemployment and Leisure

Researchers on unemployment have examined leisure as blocks of free time with unemployment being a manifestation of enforced unobliged time. Cass (1988) suggests that being unemployed means having 8 to 10 hours to fill each working day that previously would have been devoted to structured work activity. This "free time" is not equivalent to having vastly increased leisure time. She further comments that the loss of purpose, erosion of self-confidence and lack of success in job search contribute to low self-perception and motivation. In this frame of mind, the most likely reaction to increased uncommitted time is boredom. Brewer (1980) notes that as boredom and aimlessness become more acute, there is increasing likelihood that the behaviour of the unemployed will be construed as wilful indolence. Thus at a time of needing extra support and understanding, they are vulnerable to criticism.

Kelvin, Dewberry and Morley-Bunker (1984) found that the mean amount of time by unemployed males and females out of home was five hours. Most of this was spent on entertainment, followed by shopping, then active leisure which took up to one hour per day, most of it walking around the shops. The remaining 19 hours per day were spent in the home, most of this time, excluding sleep, being spent on passive entertainment, including television watching, followed by housework.

According to Hill (1978), the great killer of time for the unemployed in the seventies was almost certainly television. It is pervasive and obliterating and today even more so. Kelvin and Jarrett (1985) comment that individuals who incessantly watch television get sick of doing so, get even sicker of seeing themselves doing it. They are aware that they are merely killing time and angry, not the least with themselves, that they can find no better use of it. If unemployment induces boredom, passivity and withdrawal into the home then a second question may be raised:

How can sport and recreation ameliorate the impact of job loss?

The Benefits of Meaningful Activity

Haworth and Evans (1987) indicate that engagement in personal meaningful activity has a moderating effect on the negative psychological impact of employment. Several studies may be cited on the importance of such engagement. Hepworth (1980), studying a sample of 78 unemployed men of varying ages and occupational status, found that the best single predictor of mental health is whether or not a man feels his time is occupied. Swinburne (1981) notes that activity had a moderating effect on the negative aspects of unemployment. Of the 20 unemployed managers and professional men, 19 stressed the importance of keeping active. In the study by Fryer and Payne (1984), 11 proactive people of different socio-economic backgrounds were deemed to be coping well with unemployment as a consequence of having high levels of personal activity and the capacity to structure time. Kilpatrick and Trew (1985), who investigated how a sample of 121 unemployed men in the 25-45 age range spent their time found a significant relationship between psychological well-being and active lifestyle with a progressive decline in mental health being paralleled by decreasing activity and withdrawal into the home.

Kay (1990) studied a racially mixed subsample of men and women in Britain who were committed users of a Sports Training and Recreation Scheme (STARS) while unemployed. For them the experience of unemployment was positive, but for the majority of the main sample it was not. Kay's subsample of 18 committed STARS users had different leisure patterns from those described in most other studies. They were more self-confident, busier and more active after participation in STARS. They spent more time out of the home, had much more social contact than the average unemployed person, and took part in a wide range of different activities. The relatively high level of activity was not confined to their participation in STARS, but was evident in their lifestyle as a whole. These patterns were not continuations of previous active lifestyles. They were developed during unemployment.

Glyptis (1994) reported on a number of public provision sport and recreation schemes which met with mixed success. She concluded that sport can significantly ease the experience of unemployment for only a small minority. However, many unemployed people find sport a rewarding leisure activity to take part in occasionally, and the provision of opportunities is therefore important. She suggested that barriers that unemployed people face, such as lack of income, mobility and intangibles like loss of self esteem and purpose should be removed. Glyptis maintained that the removal of barriers could be achieved by good management, promotion, flexibility to adapt to changing needs and a willingness to work with rather than for unemployed people.

In Australia recent investigations into the lives of the unemployed have stressed the importance of public provision for sport and recreation services. The National Council for the Year of the Family (1994) suggested better access to recreational activities to improve the quality of life while seeking employment. This was important for all family members, and especially for young people. Langmore and Quiggin (1994) in their book "Work for All" suggest a national goal for a *creative society* in which vitality and liveliness are encouraged. They see leisure as an essential part of rounded living and seek government support among other things for sport and recreation.

If active lifestyles are beneficial and programs designed to promote commitment to the health and wellbeing are made available to unemployed people, then a third question could be raised:

> How can public sport and recreation programmes be delivered to young unemployed adults to promote commitment to a healthy lifestyle?

Approach and Design of the Study

This study was planned in two stages, an exploratory and a confirmatory stage. Since very little work has been done on young adults, I thought it prudent to become immersed in issues that effect their health and well-being so that I could see the steps that may be taken to be responsive to those needs. The first phase was interactive and cross-sectional and comprised the exploratory stage. It consisted of workshops with young unemployed males and females between the ages of 18 and 30. The second phase was also interactive and involved lifestyle and depth interviews with young people. Depth interviews were also conducted with providers of leisure and recreation services in order to understand the problems involved in offering programs to the unemployed.

The anonymity of persons and institutions in the study has been maintained by using pseudonyms. In this way the respective identities have been preserved and the ethics of research maintained.

Structure of the Book

The following chapter examines the recent literature on the impact of unemployment on the leisure of young people, followed by the methodology utilised in the study. Results from the workshops are reported in Chapter 4. The impact of unemployment on leisure and lifestyle from data derived from the lifestyle questionnaire are described in Chapter 5. Chapter 6 deals with depth interviews with ten males and ten females. Chapter 7 discusses the benefits and losses that arise from employment. This is followed by Chapter 8, which deals with interviews with providers of local authority leisure and recreation services. Chapter 9 sums up the study, states the findings and makes recommendations for programs that will enhance the health, leisure and lifestyle of young unemployed people.

2

Literature on Young People's Experience of Unemployment

This chapter discusses some of the recent literature on various aspects of the way in which young people experience unemployment. Starting with different perspectives of youth that have proposed, the review goes on to discuss attempts to predict the future employment status of young people; theories of the experience of unemployment; its impact on leisure; and differences between males and females in employment experience. The review concludes with the controversial questions of how unemployment results in the exclusion of young people and the ways in which they may be helped.

Perspectives of Youth

Young people are known to be unfazed by the pace of change and the technologies that give adults anxiety attacks as they learn to thrive on chaos, uncertainty and insecurity in ways their parents never have (Rushkoff, 1996). This statement may be applicable to some young people, but for others there is a much darker picture. Eckersley (1997) portrays three perspectives of youth – post-modern, conventional, and transformational. The first category is attuned to the post-modern world: adapted to its transience, fragmentation, and pluralism; comfortable with its absence of absolutes and blurred distinctions between real and unreal; at home in cyberspace as in physical space; equipped for its abundant opportunities, exciting choices and limitless freedoms – and its hazards and risks. The 'conventional' portrait suggests that most young people successfully negotiate the transitions of adolescence to become well-adjusted adults. They cherish their families, enjoy life and are confident they'll get what they want out of it. The 'transformational' portrait reveals a much darker picture where young people are cynical, alienated, pessimistic, disillusioned and disengaged. Many are confused and angry, uncertain of what the future holds and what society expects of them. There are several categories of youth that fit the 'transformational' pattern and the unemployed is one of them.

Predicting Youth Unemployment

Australian research indicates that some demographic variables may be used to predict the future employment status of young people. For example, individuals are more likely to be unemployed in the future if they come from lower economic backgrounds and have fewer educational qualifications (Lynn, Hampson and Magee, 1984), and come from a family where English is rarely spoken or where at least one family member is already unemployed (Tiggeman & Winefield, 1989).

Other studies indicate that psychological variables are also able to predict future employment status. For instance, individuals are more likely to be unemployed in the future if they report higher levels of self-blame, lower levels of optimism, utilise poor coping strategies (Leana and Feldman, 1995), indicate lower levels of conscientiousness or have little job-seeking support from family and friends (Wanberg, Watt & Rumsey, 1996).

Theories of Unemployment Experience

The psychological consequences of unemployment are not homogenous (Fryer, 1995a). There is considerable variation from person to person amongst those affected in the severity of the psychological impact of unemployment. The literature reveals several theoretical approaches to the experience of unemployment. We may focus on four that appear to be applicable to young people. They are deprivation, personal agency, rite of passage and gain-loss approaches.

With the *deprivation* approach Jahoda (1979, 1984, 1986, 1992) argues that employment promotes well-being by providing people with a time structure, social contacts, a collective purpose, a sense of identity, and regular activity. These five 'categories of experience', as she terms them, are important adjuncts to the manifest consequence of earning a living. When people are unemployed they are deprived of access to these categories of experience and the manifest function of earning a living in the social institution of employment.

The *personal agency* theory originated when Fryer and Payne (1984) undertook a study of a small group of unemployed people who were experiencing material but not psychological deprivation by adopting a proactive stance towards unemployment. Ideas and concepts of their personal agency theory (1986) were further developed by Fryer (1995b), who summarised its assumptions in two propositions. Firstly, that people are socially embedded agents actively striving for purposeful self-determination, attempting to make sense of, initiating, influencing and coping with events in line with personal values, goals and expectations of the future in a context of cultural norms, traditions and past experience. Secondly that, whilst personal agency is sometimes empowered in interaction with labour market social settings and systems, agency is frequently undermined, restricted and frustrated by formal and informal social forces. Commenting on the deprivation and personal agency approaches, Haworth (1997) concludes that Jahoda and Fryer both stress the importance for wellbeing of the psychological categories of experience. Jahoda stresses the importance of social institutions in facilitating access to these categories of experience, whilst Fryer' points to the inhibitory influence which poverty, social arrangements and cultural practices can have on personal agency, thereby restricting access to positive of experiences.

The key proposition of the *status passage* theory is that unemployment is not a static experience but a process. Unemployment is not merely a status but one stage within a transition which involves job loss (unless the person has never had a job) and reemployment (Ezzy, 1993). A status passage entails an individual's movement into a different part of the social structure, or a loss or gain of privilege, influence or power, and a changed identity and sense of self, as well as changed behaviour (Glaser and Strauss, 1971).

Attitudes towards the loss of work are known to vary. Kelly (1980) developed a *gain-loss-attachment-detachment* model (GLAD) by adding a cognitive attachment to the traditional affective gain-loss model. According to Hayes and Nutman (1981), analysis of the literature suggests that unemployment is overwhelmingly seen in terms of both detachment and attachment loss and rarely in terms of gain. For some young people loss of employment is felt so severely that they even offer to work for nothing (Baker, 1993). Apprentices are particularly vulnerable because of their need to complete their training.

Unemployment and Leisure

The role of leisure and its effect on unemployment are mixed. One view is that leisure is regarded as a vital contributor to the quality of life. Schemes for the unemployed have stimulated new participation and recruited back into sport a number of lapsed participants, but failed for most to sustain participation (Glyptis, 1994). For committed unemployed users, sports' leadership schemes did counteract many of the problems of unemployment (Kay, 1994). Studies of young unemployed adults by Evans and Haworth (1991), Haworth and Evans (1987) and Haworth and Ducker (1991) show that engagement in activity is associated with enhanced well-being, but it is less than that for a matched sample of employed people. However, not all types of leisure are able to provide access to valued experiences.

The other view that leisure does not fulfil functional alternatives for work is espoused by a number of researchers. Jahoda (1981) comments that leisure activities, from TV to sports and self-improvements are fine in themselves as complements to work, but they lack the compelling manifest function of earning a living. Guérin (1984) who conducted research on a sample of young unemployed persons (19-25) with little or no qualifications concluded that unemployment led her respondents to social isolation and made them unable to invest in any kind of personal project, including leisure activities. Roberts (1992) shows that leisure may add to the quality of life for people in employment, but it seems fundamentally incapable of providing an alternative for people without jobs. Leisure may help preserve the psychic well-being during unemployment, but is not a long-term substitute for employment (Roberts, Brodie and Dench, 1987).

The issue of whether the leisure of young people is impoverished as a result of unemployment is examined by Roberts (1997), who maintains that the range of activities is not reduced, but the frequency of participation decreases because of the lesser income. Similar conclusions are noted by Gallie, Gershuny and Vogler (1995) who found little evidence of any general tendency of the unemployed to withdraw into inactivity. They found that the general activity levels of the unemployed were very similar to those of the employed. As a consequence activities in pubs and clubs are less frequent and often done at lower cost (Roberts, 1997) or when participation in activities are unaffordable, they may be substituted by no or low cost activity (Lobo, 1996).

Unemployment and Gender

The effects of female unemployment on leisure has received little research attention, but studies by Brenner and Leui (1987) show that women's sex role means that they may be more tolerant of job loss and long term unemployment than men. Hammarstrom's (1994) work with Swedish young adults show that girls are more likely to use periods of unemployment positively than boys and Rapoport (1982) notes that women have greater experience in structuring non-work time. Kay (1997) argues that the gendered change in the labour market makes female unemployment an area ripe for investigation.

In recent years there has been one notable study which has examined the effect of unemployment from a gender perspective (Gallie et al., 1995). They found that the mean activity score of unemployed men was a little lower than employed men. Among women, however, the pattern was reversed, with the unemployed showing slightly higher scores than the employed. Men and women differ in activity patterns. There were differences in the type of activities men and women typically engaged in. Men were more likely to spend time going to the pub, while women were more likely to visit others and have people around in their homes. Men's activities may have been more costly and therefore particularly vulnerable to be curtailed in unemployment. For women, the key resource may have been time rather than money, with unemployment facilitating a slightly higher level of activity. Unemployed males and females spent a greater amount of time on passive forms of leisure than their employed counterparts. For both sexes, roughly half of the extra time in the day that had to be filled as the result of being without employment was 'passive' time. Another important difference between the employed and unemployed lay in the nature rather than the extensiveness of their networks. Those without jobs were in relatively segregated networks in which their friends also tended to be unemployed.

Unemployment and Exclusion

Prolonged unemployment leads to multidimensional disadvantage, which is of substantial duration and which involves dissociation from the major social and occupational milieus of society (Room et al., 1993). Two decades ago Townsend (1979) recognized the need to include leisure activities in the definition of poverty because deprivation includes different spheres of life – in work, at home, in travel, and in leisure time activities. Alcock (1997) believes that leisure has become a source and site of inequality. The correlation between income and leisure participation is borne out by statistics that show a decline according to occupation status (National Statistics Office, 1998).

Australian research on the effect of long term unemployment on young people shows three general impacts (Crooks, 1996). First, It forces people into a subsistence lifestyle where a limited social security payment is spread watchfully over rent, food, fuel bills, transport and children's clothing. Secondly, it causes a painful contraction of personal networks and social life as people withdraw from mainstream activity. Ironically, one of the few constant links to others is through what is perceived by many unemployed people to be a demeaning and ritualistic visit to the employment agency or the social security department. Thirdly, there is less security and more uncertainty in the lives of unemployed people – they sense the futility of a training program if there is no job at the end of it; uncertainty dominates their emotions; they don't know how they'll be managing in a few years' time; or whether they will have any security in the rest of their adult life; their spirits take a battering; they feel angry and bitter towards the nation's leaders; yet they are determined not to go under.

In the US unemployment has been linked to truancy and non-completion of schooling, family break-up, substane abuse, alienation, discrimination, illness and premature death, and poverty (Siegel, 1994). In Australia Thomson (1995) has raised the question of the diminished social status of the young unemployed, linking this to dominance of labour market criteria:

> Unfortunately, there is little reward, least of all a valued and legitimate place in society, for young people who are not employed ... when young people have a genuine desire or interest in a particular activity which does not fall under particular labour market or vocational categories, they are often discouraged from pursuing it because this type of activity does not translate into immediate economic reward ... For any person who does not neatly fit into labour market criteria, their status, identity and legitimacy as citizens is brought into question (pp 209-11).

There is little doubt that young unemployed people are excluded culturally and economically as full participating members within the community. As a consequence they are relegated to what Morris (1994) referred to as an underclass, a category of disadvantage.

People have rights. These include regular access to some form of structured social activity and rights to health protection and health promotion (Coles, 1995). Frey et al (1995) insist that 'unemployment is not only a social problem for society, and a tragedy for individual unemployed young people, it is also a violation of fundamental children's right, the right to a meaningful present leading to a meaningful future'. Brownlee (1992) believes that leisure is one of the basic human rights safeguarded by the United Nations Declaration of Human Rights, which in Article 24 states that everyone has the right to rest and leisure, including reasonable limitation of working hours and periodic holidays with pay. Article 2 of the Sao Paulo Declaration (World Leisure, 1998) states that all persons have the right to leisure through economic, political and social policies that are equitable and sustainable. However, these rights have been eroded by policies to keep leisure facilities as units of economic viability. Further, breaches of rights do not warrant a remedy in court as they cannot be viewed in a true legal sense. Thus, rights are interpreted as standards (Roche, 1997), which are often ignored. While in paid employment, young people have the means to satisfy their physiological and social needs at leisure outlets, but how can these needs be fulfilled when they are materially and psychologically disadvantaged through unemployment?

In recent times various schemes have been tried and implemented to access leisure for disadvantaged groups such as the unemployed. Collins and Kennett (1998), have reviewed the use of leisure cards for the poor, but note that the increased need for financial accountability by leisure providers has pushed into the background social objectives of providing leisure opportunities to the public in favour of better economic outcomes. The inability to pay for services and the movement away from concessionary group leisure cards excludes those who are unemployed. Haworth (1997) suggests that social inclusion through participation in work programs may enhance participation in leisure activities and produce more social activity in contrast to the withdrawn isolated lifestyles. This view is supported by MacDonald (1997), whose work on employment assistance programs for unemployed young people has resulted in improved self-esteem, extended networks and friendships, as well as training and work experience which lead to accreditation and further training. Special sport counselling programs for young offenders have helped them to refrain from crime. Nichols (1997) has shown how sporting activities can provide a medium for a process that leads to change of self-concept, involving a rejection of offending behaviour. Thus the role of leisure could lead to a positive approach and a new lifestyle.

If social exclusion has been used as an overarching concept for accessibility, financial, identity, cultural, technological and self exclusions, then the observations and inferences derived from the research into unemployment must conclude that job loss causes social exclusion for many. That being the case, it must also be concluded that unemployment is an impediment to leisure and human development. However, no studies have been conducted to show the quantity and types of losses incurred or if there are any gains to be made by job loss. The question therefore arises: Is youth unemployment an impediment or catalyst to leisure and human development?

If social exclusion has been used as an overarching concept for accessibility, financial, identity, cultural, technological and self exclusions, then the observations and inferences derived from the research into unemployment must conclude that job loss causes social exclusion for many. That being the case, it must also be concluded that unemployment is an impediment to leisure and human development. However, no studies have been conducted to show the quantity and types of losses incurred or if there are any gains to be made by job loss. The question therefore arises: Is youth unemployment an impediment or catalyst to leisure and human development? An examination to leisure service delivery might give a few clues as to whether the unemployed are included or not.

Leisure Service Delivery

Over the past fifty years, the leisure service delivery paradigm has been characterised by several approaches. They include: community service and development; marketing and commercial; humanitarian and humanistic; benefits based; social action; compulsory competitive tendering; and best value.

In its early formulations "recreation and park administration" was community service based. It was viewed as an important governmental function, one that had the potential for considerable good within a community. As early as 1948, Meyer and Brightbill succinctly summarised this approach as:

> Recreation had no peer, with the possible exception of a desirable family environment, in strengthening and preserving the best in children and youth stabilising family and community living...It is the first line of opportunity in preventing social ills...(pp. 6-7).

This approach characterised recreation and leisure service delivery in the United States and Australia during the 1960s and 70s. Human service was seen as the essential function of government, and although various agencies and organisations might have specific human service functions, delivery was based on linkages between agencies to provide a broader base of services than any one agency could provide (Niepoth, 1983). It came to be known as the community development approach.

During the 1980s there was a change in the prevailing philosophy of leisure service delivery. A declining tax base, inflation, and increased operational costs made it necessary for many leisure service agencies to make dramatic cutbacks. Along with these austerity measures came a more business-oriented approach to leisure service. Modelled after commercial recreation ventures, public agencies began to adopt a "marketing approach" (Howard and Crompton, 1980; Crompton, 1987) to service delivery. Torkildsen (1992) summarised this change:

> Public sector marketing is a hybrid of approaches which evolved historically and are caught up with commercial approaches, primarily to limit subsidy or help the facilities pay for themselves (p.343).

Perhaps the main weakness of the marketing approach to leisure is that it is based on a logical positivistic philosophy that is clearly materialistic and linear in nature. Such a philosophy takes a narrow view of leisure, viewing it in quantitative terms. This perspective, born out of the Puritan Work Ethic, subscribes to the notion that leisure is discretionary or excess time. From this perspective, the leisure service agency is primarily concerned with marketing activities and programs that have appeal to the paying public. Murphy (1980) warned about this approach to service delivery:

> Utilising a discretionary time perspective as the only philosophical basis for leisure service programming is nearsighted. It serves only to keep people where they are; it perpetuates the myth of an industrial rhythm of life; it limits the development of human potential and reduces the prospects for a high standard of quality of life...(p.198).

What Murphy was calling for was a humanistic approach to leisure service delivery. He argued that leisure service should be concerned not just with the provision of leisure activities, but with human and community development. His view of a leisure service was expansive and holistic. For Murphy leisure service had to include the remediation of factors that prevented individuals from meaningful involvement in the community, limited their capacity for self-expression, and hindered their opportunities for rich and varied leisure experiences.

The harsh economic reality of the 1980s in the Western world did little to promote Murphy's view of humanistic leisure service delivery. The marketing model seemed to predominate the thinking of most planners throughout the 1980s. With the 1990s came the realisation that the business approach to public recreation was eroding the place of the recreation professional. Godbey warned that unless leisure service included a humanistic component, it would soon "cease to exist..." (Kraus, 1997, p.389).

In Australia reforms in the name of economic rationalism have failed to increase choices for most people or to fulfil the utilitarian principle of the greatest happiness for the greatest number. They have failed to redistribute income equally. Instead, there has been a significant redistribution of income upwards; that is, the rich have got richer (Pusey, 1991). The counterfeit of economic rationalism is massive unemployment. Unemployment not only causes economic disadvantage to children, but they also experience the trauma their parents are going through (Langmore and Quiggin, 1994). The recreation of these children is adversely affected (Lobo and Watkins, 1995). Young unemployed males and females are restricted in their leisure as a result of material, psychological and social deprivation (Lobo, 1997). Other disadvantaged segments of society face similar problems. Consequently, some leisure scholars have denounced the market approach. Roberts (1999) notes that the market experience has been a proven failure in the promise of a satisfying life. He suggests that we are driven more powerfully by more socially induced wants than by a more basic nature. Parker (1999) believes that people who use their leisure capital creatively and pleasurably, by themselves or in the company of others have better leisure experiences than those who turn to the market to consume leisure as a commodity.

In the United States, there is a blending of the old and the new. The human services approach is coming together with the marketing approach to produce a more benefits based delivery system. Although not full-circle, this return to a more humanitarian perspective has produced in some leisure service agencies a promising blend of the best elements from the marketing orientation with the social commitment of the early community development model. But when it comes to the needs of the invisible minority, such as the unemployed, this new hybrid model of leisure management may not be enough. Perhaps another dimension needs to be added to the mix – social action.

The main attribute of social action is advocacy, and this essentially means to champion a cause or group. Edginton, Hanson, Edginton and Hudson (1998) describe the social action strategy:

> It presumes that there is a disadvantaged population, great injustice, and a need to force the system, institutions, organisations, and agencies to change the ways they are distributing resources, hence services (p.39).

Edginton et al. (1998) believe that a leisure service agency can serve as an agent for social change in several ways. Advocacy can be identified by several roles (Edginton and Compton, 1975). Initiator, planner and organiser roles identify the problem, serve as a catalyst and outline a plan of action. The investigator role calls for organising facts and information in support of the group or cause. Help in resolving disputes between the disadvantaged and others can be achieved through the negotiator role. The lobbyist represents the needs of the disadvantaged by influencing decision-makers to make decisions favourable to the disadvantaged group. Counsellor and resource specialists can match individuals and groups with resources and help facilitate desired changes. The educator role assists with awareness of the plight of the disadvantaged and educating the disadvantaged to utilise resources that help themselves. Evaluation steps can be used to determine the degree of change that has occurred and if necessary new strategies that might be introduced to further newly introduced intended changes.

In the 1980s and the early 1990s the need for the leisure market to become more competitive brought in a new approach to service delivery through Compulsory Competitive Tendering (CCT). With increasing consumerism and competition as a result of CCT, leisure managers had to win CCT contracts and had to meet requirements of CCT specifications. In order to be competitive leisure managers had to adopt quality management procedures and deliver quality programs (Robinson, 2000). Economy, efficiency and effectiveness were the performance indicators of CCT (Williams, 2000).

The flow-on from CCT was the Best Value approach that took hold in the late 1990s and into the new millennium. Through Best Value local authorities are expected to search continuously "... to improve the quality, efficiency and effectiveness of all its services ..." (ILAM, 1997: p.1). Driven by the need to monitor service performance, Best Value relies on the 4Cs principle of challenge, compare, consult and compete. The new approaches are laudable and appropriate for citizens who have the ability to pay for services. But what about those who seek value, but do not have the means?

Helping the Young Unemployed

Along with recognition of the plight of the young unemployed, there are doubtless well-meaning attempts to help the individuals concerned. There is a small self-help literature, exemplified by Heathwood (1992), who has compiled a collection of suggestions under the dubious title of *Back on Top. Finding Yourself. Finding a Job.* She writes about knockbacks that are very likely to be experienced by the young unemployed:

> Each time you are turned down you will feel some of the same agony that you felt when you are retrenched. Be aware that this is normal and that it will not do you any long-term harm ...

This sort of 'advice', besides being almost flippantly patronising, is calculated to reconcile young people to a fate that, far from being inevitable, is socially constructed.

The other side of happiness when finding a job (a comparatively rare event) is a feeling of guilt when failing to find one (a common event). One of the young unemployed (Storer, 1998), sums this up well: "There's a view that anyone can find a job if they try hard enough. Not true. I've knocked on hundreds of doors. For all that effort, I still feel guilty.'

Another motive for helping the young unemployed is fear of the damage that they can do in their revolt against a society that has badly let them down. As Watts (2000) puts it, 'prolonged high unemployment poses a serious threat to the social and economic fabric of our society.' Durrance and Hughes (1996) deplore the 'aggressive costumes and manners' that some young unemployed display. But those authors do recognise that many are 'unhappy children who are often in poor physical and mental health. They are seeking support that they rarely find.'

3

Methodology

The methods used in the study are described in this chapter. There were two phases – exploratory and confirmatory. The exploratory phase comprised group discussions and the confirmatory phase included the administration of the lifestyle questionnaire, depth interviews with young males and females and providers of sport and recreation services. The later section of the chapter deals with data collection and analysis.

Procedure and Population

The exploratory stage: This study focused on unemployed male and female young adults between the ages of 18 and 30. This phase consisted of five workshops at which substantial group discussions took place. Access to these groups was made possible through training programs conducted at State and Federal levels. The Western Australian Department of Training had adopted a State Employment Assistance Strategy which conducted training programs through Job Link agencies. Projects such as the Youth Access Scheme (YAS) was one of several Job Link undertakings. The Department of Employment, Education and Training (DEET) conducted The

Landcare and Environment Action Program (LEAP), which was a Commonwealth initiative to provide opportunities for young Australians to enhance their vocational skills and their opportunities for further vocational training and employment. DEET also sponsored labour training programs under Skillshare projects and although these programs encompassed the whole job-seeking spectrum, there were several programs which attracted young adults. Training programs also targeted certain groups, such as youth at risk, long term unemployed, women returning to the workforce, aborigines, ex-offenders, people with disabilities and migrants.

The purpose of the discussions was to identify health, sport and recreation issues facing young unemployed people. This was done by questions put to participants on the impact of unemployment on self and on sport and recreation. Issues such as barriers to participation were examined in some detail (Appendix A). Each session lasted for three hours with a half hour break. Comments made by the participants in response to a question were recorded on butcher's paper, displayed at the front on a flip-chart and were readable by all. At the conclusion of comments the problem was evaluated. Special care was taken to state and distinguish what generally applied to the group and what applied to individuals who may or may not have experienced the problems of the majority. There was an emphasis on similarity as well as differences.

Of the five group discussion sessions, attempts were made to conduct at least two sessions in the country towns. Job training agencies gave full support to the group discussion sessions. The sessions were promoted as "Coping with Unemployment" workshops, where the participants were encouraged to design personal plans to incorporate sport and recreation into a healthy lifestyle.

The confirmatory stage: The second aspect of the study and the start of the confirmatory phase was by the administration of a retrospective lifestyle questionnaire.

Questionnaires were given to all participants in the group discussions and others were distributed at job training offices. Instructions were left with relevant personnel that the questionnaires were to be completed by unemployed persons under 30 years of age. Broad areas were studied including the impact of unemployment on self, participation in sport and recreation, barriers to participation and commitment to a healthy lifestyle (Appendix B). The return rate of the self-administered questionnaire was very small. Consequently, interviews were conducted and audio-taped. The self-administered questionnaires and the interview responses totalled 82 respondents.

A purposeful sample of 20 individuals, 10 male and 10 female were selected and interviewed in depth (Appendix C) to provide information-rich material of central importance to the study (Patton, 1987). Since the problem was determining the impact of unemployment and the effects of job loss on the health and well-being of individuals concerned, a great deal would be learned by focusing in depth on a small number of carefully selected individuals rather than gathering little information from a large, statistically significant sample.

A subsidiary sample was used to study the question of employment benefits and losses. In February 1999, 44 young people between the ages of 18 and 30 volunteered to be interviewed at job training venues. The interviews were audio-taped and later transcribed. There were 28 (64%) males and 16 females (36%). Twenty-four were between the ages of 18 and 24 years and 20 were between 25 and 30 years. Questions were asked on: the benefits and losses of employment; and activities before and after job loss in the home, for fitness, sociability, and entertainment. Frequencies of activities before and after job loss were recorded. In this way it was possible to know whether leisure activities were continued or discontinued after unemployment. If they were discontinued or continued more intensely, then it could be inferred that unemployment was an impediment or a catalyst respectively to leisure and human development. Audio tape recordings in a few cases were undecipherable and in some cases the respondents failed to answer a question. Spoiled responses resulted in fewer than the maximum of 44 responses. In order to protect the anonymity of the participants, pseudonyms were assigned.

Nine providers of sport and recreation services were selected to be interviewed in-depth (Appendix D) to examine strategies to deliver services taking into account the material and psychological deprivations of the unemployed. Special attention was paid to the removal of barriers to participation and sensitivity towards the management, promotion and flexibility to varying and changing needs of the unemployed as well as the providers. The nine providers included recreation coordinators and senior officers in local authorities in the Perth Metropolitan area and at least two on the City-rural fringe.

Data Collection and Analysis

Qualitative data were collected and analysed for the exploratory and confirmatory stages using a Non-numerical Unstructured Data Indexing, Searching and Theorising (NUDIST) software package (Richards, 1992).

Information from group discussions was processed by inductive and content analysis. Through inductive analysis, patterns, themes, and categories that emerged were identified for similarity and variation. The content was assembled, condensed, organised and classified into themes arising from the data (Patton, 1987). Raw data on butcher's paper from group discussions, audio-taped information from in-depth interviews and responses from the lifestyle questionnaires were word processed before being organised for thematic categorisation into the NUDIST program. Elementary statistics were used to compare variations between and within characteristics being studied. These statistics included frequencies, percentages, the mode to identify central tendency and the range to show differences.

In the retrospective lifestyle questionnaire, particular attention was paid to leisure behaviour as it related to sport and recreation. Activities were categorised as in-the-home and out-of-home. The out-of-home activities were further grouped into fitness, socialising, entertainment, and club/association membership. Before and After Unemployment categories were set for each grouping of sport and recreation activity. Before/After responses were dichotomised in order that the data reveal changes that occur or do not occur in leisure behaviour as a result of unemployment. The category of in-the-home activity was dichotomised on a *high/low* basis. Thus high participation in the home before unemployment and low participation after unemployment was a *high/low* response. The in-the-home category had four possibilities on a before/after basis: *high/high; high/low; low/high* and *low/low*. Similarly, fitness, socialising, entertainment and club/association membership had dichotomous before/after categories of leisure behaviours labelled as: *active/passive; involved/uninvolved; frequent/infrequent;* and *retained/discontinued* respectively. Like the activity-in-the-home category, leisure behaviour had four possibilities on a before/after basis of unemployment. A similar design used to measure effects of unemployment on the leisure behaviour of mature-aged adults had proved to be very convincing, valid and reliable.

Eighty-two young people attending labour market programs between the ages of 18 and 30 volunteered to be interviewed. They consisted of 49 (60%) males and 33 (40%) females. Of the males 33 (67%) were between the ages of 18 and 24 years, and 16 (33%) between 25 and 30 years. Among the females 25 (76%) were between 18 and 24 and 8 (24%) between 25 and 30 years.

Educational levels were categorised as lower secondary, which is up to Year 10 of high school, upper secondary, Year 12, the final year of high school, and tertiary, which included technical and further education beyond high school or university studies. The number of males with lower secondary education was 23 (47%), upper secondary, 14 (29%) and tertiary 12 (24%). Among the females, the proportions were 11 (33%), 10 (30%) and 12 (37%) respectively. Of the total of 82 participants, three (all females) had university bachelor degrees.

On a self-perceived financial scale from comfortable to very poor, males rated themselves in the following way: comfortable 15 (31%), poor 26 (53%), and very poor 8 (16%). Among females the proportions were: comfortable 10 (30.5%), poor 13 (39%), and very poor 10 (30.5%).

Previous employment history was categorised as intermittent, steady and no previous employment. Among the males, 23 (55%) had intermittent, 17 (40%) steady, and 2 (5%) had no previous employment. Proportions for females were: intermittent 13 (42%) and steady 18 (58%). There were no female cases of no previous employment.

Questions put to young people focused on: impact of job loss; job search efforts; relationships with the family; the effect on leisure in and out of home; personal goals; personal resources; and external resources. Out-of-home categories include activities for fitness, sociability, and entertainment and membership in clubs and associations.

Elementary statistical measures have been utilised to show similarities and divergences. The mean is used to show the number of activities young people participated in before unemployment. Where the number of activities in and out of the home exceeds four, Kendall's Coefficient of Concordance (Siegel and Castellan, 1988) is used to indicate agreement or otherwise of participation rates between males and females. Where the number of activities is four or less, comparisons are made on a percentage basis. Since participants' responses of activities in each of the leisure categories may be more than one, percentages are calculated on the basis of the total number of responses. The number of responses exceeds the number of respondents.

In-depth interviews with the twenty individuals were audio-taped and transcribed to computer disk ready for introduction into the NUDIST project. Masses of seemingly formless data were broken down into text units, each of which were indexed under categories of impact of on self, various sub-categories of leisure activity, barriers to participation and preferred and actual lifestyle patterns in unemployment and employment. A text unit was made up of a word, phrase or paragraph conveying an idea or perception leading to categories of the unemployment experience, but most texts units were in paragraph form. With the aid of the NUDIST project, indexed data in text unit form was easily searched and retrievable to make comparisons, identify effects, differences and similarities, observe impacts of varying degrees and establishing linkages. Text units were also searched and retrieved in category sequence for a single interview or a set of personal interviews through the NUDIST search and retrieval capability.

Categorised data were analysed at two levels – functional and interpretative (Hedges, 1987). At the functional level content analysis for patterns, themes and categories emerged inductively from the data. At the interpretative level, meanings associated with the text were sought. The textual analysis focused on looking for patterns and understandings within texts of the interview material (Henderson, 1991). Content analysis and textual analysis were used to answer the research questions raised in the study.

Limitations of the Study

It was planned that ten group discussion sessions would be held, with one aboriginal and two migrant groups. Instead five were held and in one there was a high representations of indigenous people. In all others young migrants were well represented. Several attempts were made to hold workshops in Kalgoorlie and Karratha, but job training agencies failed to attract unemployed young people to attend. Hence no groups met in those towns. However, viable numbers met in the South West towns of Bunbury and Albany.

Many young people preferred being interviewed rather than completing a lifestyle questionnaire. Therefore the structured questionnaire with open ended questions sought verbal responses which were audio taped and then transcribed. This mode of data collection induced some powerful data, which would otherwise have been missed had respondents completed a hand-written questionnaire. The interview format enriched the quality of the study. There were some disappointing attendances at workshop and interview sessions, as often young people failed to turn up. Many promised to attend, but few were present.

It was also planned that 20 young people would be selected from those who completed the questionnaire. Tracking those who were selected was extremely difficult. Contact was lost with most of them. It was therefore decided to interview in depth ten males and ten females who were unemployed and who had not participated in the lifestyle questionnaire phase. These young people were interviewed once and not twice as originally planned. The difficulties of tracking these young people for a second interview was a huge problem. As it turned out the quality of data that accrued was what was hoped for.

Ten providers of sport and recreation services were to be interviewed. The final number was nine as one provider had gone on leave and was unavailable. All nine providers were coordinators of local authorities. Development officers of sports' associations and voluntary organisations were not included.

4

Workshops on
Unemployment and Leisure

This chapter attempts to seek the views of young people on how losing their job affected their leisure. By interacting with young people I hoped that issues would emerge which would be used in the lifestyle questionnaire and depth interviews in the later phases of the study. Five workshops were held in Fremantle, Wanneroo, Midland, Albany and Bunbury. The numbers in each workshop ranged from 20 in Fremantle to 7 in Wanneroo. Midland had 19, Albany and Bunbury 8 each.

I held discussions with all participants in a single group. The questions dealt with: the type of person individuals were before unemployment; the impact of unemployment; leisure activities before unemployment; effects on leisure after job loss; impact on the family; how others – government and voluntary agencies – could lend support; and how individuals could help themselves.

The workshop discussions are reported in two ways – text and tables. When it was possible to count frequencies by a show of hands for instance, numerals have been inserted in table cells. On several occasions participants raised issues, which may or may not have had peer support. In these instances, the existence of responses is indicated by a bullet in table cells. If issues were not raised or mentioned by some of the groups, the respective cells have been left blank. Frequencies and percentages are also included in text by numerals in brackets. As far as possible words and phrases spoken by participants have been used for descriptive and anecdotal reporting.

Type of Person before Unemployment

Participants were asked: "What type of person were you before unemployment?" A range of answers was given, including: energetic, busy, happy; laidback; felt secure; bored, lazy, unhappy; artistic; and sporting. The frequency of responses is shown in Table 4.1.

Table 4.1
Type of Person before Unemployment

Type of behaviour	Fremantle	Wanneroo	Midland	Albany	Bunbury	Total	Percent
Energetic, busy, happy	8	2	12	8	8	38	45
Laidback	8	-	4	-	2	14	16
Felt secure	-	-	-	3	7	10	12
Bored, lazy, unhappy	-	3	6	-	-	9	11
Artistic	8	-	-	-	-	8	9
Sporting	6	-	-	-	-	6	7
Total responses	30	5	22	11	17	85	100

In describing themselves as energetic, busy and happy, participants used words like "confident", "good self-esteem", "busy and confident". Many said they had a sense of purpose and feelings of wellbeing. Some spoke of social and physical mobility, which meant the ability to travel from place to place and meet friends. Before unemployment there was a general feeling of happiness which augured well for physical and emotional health. Forty-five percent of the responses indicated that paid employment facilitated expending energy and being busy, both of which resulted in being happy.

Sixteen percent of responses indicated that some young people especially from the Fremantle, Midland, Bunbury groups were 'laidback' before job loss. What they meant by being laidback was that they were "hassle free" and "not bored".

Feelings of security (12%) were confined to the Albany and Bunbury groups. Feeling secure was both physical and social. Paid employment gave a "feeling of security about the future", you were "able to plan with money coming in". Others "felt more independent", "financially carefree", with "fewer personal problems". A participant from Bunbury "felt good about earning money and paying for goods", while her colleague "could plan and realise plans". Incomes meant that "there were goals and purpose in life". The social aspects of security were seen in comments such as having "a lot more friends to confide in – work friends and those outside work". It appeared that employment induced "good social support" and "good family relationships".

It was disappointing to note that some in the Wanneroo (3) and Midland (6) groups felt bored, lazy and unhappy before losing their job. None of the respondents were able to say why they felt that way. Those who felt artistic (8) and sporting (6) were solely from the Fremantle group. There may have been some bias in the artistic and sporting responses when compared to other groups, as the young people in Fremantle were involved in woodwork and creative activity and but many of them were also involved in sport as their main leisure activity.

The six categories of responses indicate that while in employment 89 percent of young people in the workshops were energetic, busy, happy, laidback secure, sporting and artistic. Sadly, there were a few (11%) who were bored, lazy and unhappy before losing their job.

Impact of Unemployment

When asked what the impact of unemployment was on them, the carefree and wellbeing feelings changed to negative and unfavourable perceptions and experiences. The responses indicated: shock, anger, frustration; bored, lazy, depressed; being a victim; low motivation; low self-esteem, confidence; and acceptance of job loss. The frequency of responses for each of the categories is in Table 4.2.

Table 4.2
Impact of Unemployment

Job Loss Impact	Fremantle	Wanneroo	Midland	Albany	Bunbury	Total	Percent
Shock, anger, frustration	15	3	5	3	5	31	21
Bored, lazy, depressed	16	6	6	7	2	37	25
Felt a victim	16	-	-	3	8	27	18
Low motivation	11	4	-	-	2	17	11
Low self esteem, confidence	16	5	-	6	3	30	20
Acceptance of job loss	-	1	7	-	-	8	5
Total responses	74	19	18	19	20	150	100

Across all the workshops, shock, anger and frustration (21%) resulted from job loss. The words angry (20) and frustration (15) were most frequently used. Feelings of revenge (4) were aroused as well as shock and disappointment. In one case, a young man experienced "initial relief – followed by uncertainty". Another felt "lost and shocked". One response indicated "no future – took a while to sink in especially when money ran out". There was no doubt that many felt traumatised as a result of job loss.

Losing their job resulted in 25 percent of respondents being bored, lazy and depressed. Here again these feelings were consistent across the groups. Seventeen responses indicated laziness, this was followed by boredom (16), depression (11) and fear (4). Other single responses included: sick physically and mentally; change of mood with friends; sad; like a bereavement; and no idea what help was available.

Eighteen percent young people in the workshops saw themselves as victims. The view of others of themselves were: thought by others as dole bludgers (16); going nowhere (11); others look down on you (11). Added to these perceptions were single responses for: "rejection and hurt"; "targeted for crime"; "intimidated"; and "wanted to do nothing with the workplace".

With the foregoing perceptions on how others in the community view jobless young people, it was no surprise that 20 percent of the responses indicated low self esteem and confidence. People felt "loss of confidence", being "inefficient", "loss of credibility", "heightened consciousness", "stigma", "loss of identity", "blow to self esteem" and "role uncertainty with spouse".

Impact on the Family

When asked what the impact of unemployment was on the family, the participants gave a whole range of responses. These were categorised as: seen as a misfit; expected to look for work; guilt doing an enjoyable activity; expected to do more jobs; arguments over trivialities; and unfavourable comparison with siblings. Since frequencies of responses were not noted, a bullet in the cells in Table 4.3 indicates that a comment was made relating to the category from the family perspective. The dash in cells indicates that the issue was not raised.

Table 4.3
Impact on the Family

Family Perspectives	Fremantle	Wanneroo	Midland	Albany	Bunbury
Seen as a misfit	●	●	●	●	●
Expected to look for work	●	-	-	-	●
Guilt doing an enjoyable activity	●	-	-	●	-
Expected to do more jobs	●	●	●	-	-
Arguments over trivialities	●	●	●	-	●
Compared with siblings	●	-	-	-	●

The 'misfit' label was expressed in the comment of "being around the house seen as a nuisance". At least fourteen participants agreed with that perception. Disappointment at being jobless (6) and ungratefulness (3) were terms used by parents about their children's predicament. One parent was reported as being disappointed with her daughter but blamed herself for the daughter's situation. Another put the ungrateful label on the daughter after providing an "education and money invested in the best school". Phrases like being "bloody nagged and nagged" were used frequently. As a consequence some participants "are home when parents are out and out when parents are at home". Others chose "being on your own". One young female smoked more cigarettes. When jobless, workshop participants were a "target of aversive comments". They were "thought as second best", "lazy", "worthless", and tagged with the "dole bludger image". It was not surprising then, that some "hid unemployment from (the) family". One young man reported that "batteries were taken out of remote to restrict television viewing".

Responses from the Fremantle and Bunbury groups indicated that they were expected to look for work. Some were "being hassled to get a job". One female was "seen as lazy compared to (her) sister". Complaints such as "get off your arse, do something" and the "longer (you) are out of (a) job the more difficult (it is) to secure one" were not unusual. Such comments made these young people "guilty (of participating) if the activity is seen to be enjoyable".

Many were expected to do more jobs in the home. One person told of "many irritable things to do all listed e.g. ironing, vacuuming, feed the pet, clean the windows". A young man reported that the "list of jobs (was) given when half asleep so all do not register". Other methods parents used were to "phone from work to check if jobs are done", "pointing out things to be done", "giving odd jobs" and putting a "list of jobs on the board to do".

Joblessness led to disharmony in the home. One participant said that "arguments over dishes lead to major fights". It was not unusual for "small things to become problems", for "comments (to) become demeaning". A young man said that his "truck driver father gives instructions on Tuesday of jobs to do, phones on Friday to inquire whether (they are) completed". The family is often blamed for disrupting the day when arguments arise, with constant reminders by siblings about job status and comments which "make you feel an instant loser".

The Fremantle and Bunbury groups pointed out that some of them were compared to their siblings. One young lady was compared to her sister as a model to be like. Another was told that she would turn out to be like her sister, who was also unemployed. Comparisons with siblings made some participants uncomfortable and led to "poor relations with sisters and parents".

Other comments not categorised in Table 4.3 were that "friends can be generally supportive" but other "friends can frown on you for not working". Many felt that they were "looked at as being different". For some, moving out the house was a preferred option to avoid the family. Participants complained that "older people can't understand why you are not employed ... they don't understand the requirements for a job in the present situation". Some admitted that parents worry about the "survival of the young". They "feel the guilt themselves" and often attribute the "sense of failure, anxiety, and being critical and judgemental" to themselves.

Leisure Activities before Unemployment

In attempting to find out about leisure activities before unemployment, young people in the workshops were asked to say what the activities they participated in. The responses were categorised into: television/video; team sports; individual activities; social activities; and music, arts and reading. The frequency of responses is in Table 4.4.

Table 4.4
Leisure Activities before Unemployment

Activities before unemployment	Fremantle	Wanneroo	Midland	Albany	Bunbury	Total	Percent
Television/ video	16	7	15	8	8	54	13
Team sports	34	7	14	3	2	60	14
Individual activities	58	11	36	14	22	141	33
Social activities	16	12	55	17	3	103	24
Music arts, reading	25	3	13	22	2	65	16
Total responses	149	40	133	64	37	423	100

Some activities mentioned are not included in the above table. They are smoking cigarettes, smoking pot, shopping and cooking. There were a total of 423 responses from 62 participants, so the average number of leisure activities per person was 6.8. This figure for activities in and out of the home is standard for Australian young people.

Of the 62 participants, 54 watched television or viewed videos. There were a small number in the Fremantle (4) and Midland (4) groups that did not indicate television and video as a leisure activity. Participants were fully involved in team sports which included: basketball (17); football (15); netball (8); rugby (8); soccer (7); hockey (3); and volleyball (1).

A wide range of individual activities was listed. Swimming (21), push bike riding (17), motor bike riding (17) and fishing (16) were followed in frequency by gym and aerobics (15), computer activities (13), camping (13), surfing (10), horse riding, rally driving, gardening (4), abseiling (3), jogging, golf (2), rollerblading, boating, doing up cars, parasailing and bungee jumping.

Social activities included: visits to pubs (21); parties (19); playing pool (18); hanging around with friends (17); telephoning friends, darts, barbecues (6); and computer arcade (1). There was also much interest in music, the arts and reading. Listening to music (21) was followed by night clubs, bands and concerts (16), reading (13), concerts and theatre (4) and singing and dancing (2). The range and forms of various types of leisure stated indicates that young people before unemployment were active, involved in the leisure domain, and generally pursued healthy lifestyles through sport and recreation.

Effects on Leisure after Job Loss

When asked how losing their job affected their leisure, young people did not did not talk in terms of activities as they did in the previous section. They spoke of how their behaviour changed as a result of the deprivation of unemployment and the increase of enforced free time. The effects mentioned were:

TV viewing increased; less of active sports; more low cost activities; more time in bed; increase in smoking and drinking; decrease in smoking and drinking; more time for fitness; longer time to do tasks; and more time with friends. The effects of unemployment are listed in Table 4.5.

Table 4.5
Effects on Leisure after Job Loss

Unemployment Effects	Fremantle	Wanneroo	Midland	Albany	Bunbury
TV viewing increased	●	●	●	●	●
Less of active sports	●	-	●	●	●
More low cost activities	-	-	●	●	●
More home activities	●	-	●	●	●
More time in bed	●	●	●	-	-
Increase in smoking/drinking	●	-	●	-	●
Decrease in smoking/drinking	-	-	●	●	-
More time for fitness	●	●	-	-	-
Longer time to do tasks	●	-	-	●	-
More time with friends	●	●	-	-	●

As many as 27 of the 62 participants reported spending more time watching television. It was interesting to hear one female stating that "often the stereo and TV are going on at the same time in the same room". At least two persons said that they watched the movies and stayed up late.

At least 19 of the 62 had reduced their participation in active sports. The reasons given were "because of the lack of money". They found it "hard to commit yourself to a team" and "borrowing money was not the answer". For some less or no participation in active sports, meant substituting with low cost activities. Walking was often mentioned (14) and one young man with more time on his hands took "longer walks with the dog as a substitute activity". A wide array of activities and comments was noted. They included: fishing; occasional visit to the pub; juggle with bill, to postpone paying to go out to a movie; walk the dog instead of swimming; hired fewer videos; riding bike; budget tightening – fix the car (myself); netball because mum pays for it; and computer games at home.

The home was the place where more time was spent on activities (11). Some took to cleaning, talking on the phone (9), others played music (8) and a few took to gardening (4). One young female took to gardening to grow "veges' for survival. Many said they spent more time in bed. At the Fremantle workshop an 18 year old young man said that on weekdays he slept till noon, then watched TV till 1.30 after which he went with friends till 6.00 pm. He came home for dinner at and went out again at 7.00 pm, only to return at 11.00 pm.

There were participants from Fremantle, Midland and Bunbury who reported and increase in alcohol consumption and smoking. The two from Midland said they had "more visits to the pub" and the one from Bunbury said, "no pub but buy bottles from shop and drink with anyone". The two who decreased drinking and smoking did so because they could not afford to indulge as much as before unemployment.

It was interesting to note that seven respondents said that their fitness had increased. Six were from Fremantle and one from Wanneroo. All did more surfing than before unemployment. When in jobs they could only go surfing during the weekend, but now they went weekdays as well.

Some participants from Fremantle and Albany spoke of taking a longer time to complete tasks after losing their job. This line of thinking emerged from one individual in each of the groups and others participating seemed to agree by nodding heads and even contributing to the discussion. Comments such as we "postpone doing things" or "did less housework but took longer" confirmed a "don't care attitude (with) cups not washed" and "lack of personal hygiene". The routine of employment was substituted by "lack of routine, passivity and boredom" where "house chores (are) forced".

The boredom of the home encouraged some participants from Fremantle, Wanneroo and Bunbury to spend more time with friends. While "hanging around with friends", "alcohol, drugs and smoking" were shared activities. Females kept in touch with friends on the phone, "visited (them) more" in order to "relieve boredom". However, there were at least three responses which indicated visiting friends less.

Help from Others

Participants were asked how others – government bodies and voluntary agencies – could help to maintain healthy lifestyles. Many ideas were mentioned, which were grouped under headings of: supply of information; access to leisure; access to training; and volunteer activity (Table 4. 6).

Table 4.6
How Others Can Help

Sources of help	Fremantle	Wanneroo	Midland	Albany	Bunbury
Supply of information	●	-	-	-	●
Access to leisure	●	-	●	●	●
Access to training	●	-	●	●	●
Volunteer activity	●	●	●	●	-

On the subject of information supply, participants suggested a booklet listing leisure activities that were cheaper. They thought that people should be made aware of what is available. They also suggested that young people's views be taken into account in meeting their needs. Bands and concerts which young people are interested in are catered for by commercial outlets. They are expensive and unaffordable. They said that less flash programs could be supplied by local authorities and clubs that young people could use.

Many hoped for concessions to access leisure programs and services. These could be offered at off peak periods. There was a suggestion that the Ministry of Sport and Recreation should sponsor programs for the unemployed and advertise these schemes at employment agencies, inviting people to play.

Access to training was geared to acquiring good leisure and work skills. The Landcare and Environment Action Program (LEAP) was seen as being most useful. Concessions to diving and other training courses would be appreciated by people who want to participate, but were unable to do so because of costs. There was a plea for less paperwork from social security, less alienation through bureaucratic structures and demoralising work, and assistance to learn new skills. Access to training could be facilitated by: cheaper or fast access to training, lower period to qualify; and concessions for travel and entry to facilities.

Participants were encouraged to involve themselves in volunteer activity. This sector could do much to increase personal motivation, experience, training, and confidence. Routines could be developed and dole bludging preconceptions removed. Volunteer activity was seen as an opportunity for future employment. The volunteer sector was considered an excellent environment for young people to learn and test their work skills to make them ready for jobs.

Helping Oneself

In an attempt to find out how jobless young people can help themselves, participants were asked how they could help themselves in making life more tolerable. Many were forthcoming with suggestions about self-help. Their responses indicated: getting a job; attending a training course; setting personal goals; mixing with others; and keeping busy. Table 4.7 lists these responses for all groups, except Albany. This was the last question on the schedule. The Albany facility had to close just before I was able to consider this issue of helping oneself, so the question was inadvertently not discussed.

Most participants felt that getting a job was the best way of making life better, even if they had to "aim lower". There were indications at all times that the thing they wanted most was a job. In all four workshops dealing with this question, participants saw the value of "attend(ing) a training course", "going back to school", and "getting a licence and qualifications". Individuals offered advice - "learn a skill", "save money while on a course", "get a qualification", "do a course" and "attend labour market programs".

Table 4.7
Helping Oneself to Make Life Better

Helping yourself	Fremantle	Wanneroo	Midland	Albany	Bunbury
Get a job	●	●	●	-	-
Attend a training course	●	●	●	-	●
Set personal goals	●	●	-	-	●
Mix with others	●	●	●	-	-
Keep busy	●	●	●	-	●

Some saw the importance of setting personal goals. There were suggestions to develop a sense of purpose, set goals, be self motivated, get involved in low or no cost activity, stay positive and improve oneself.

Mixing with others was thought to enhance self esteem and identity. By getting involved with sport, participants would meet people and make friends. Volunteering was seen as worthwhile and getting out of the home was a good diversion.

There were responses which indicated that keeping busy had made life tolerable. One was to keep active even if it had to be self enforced. Setting a routine and sticking to it was seen as useful. It was suggested that to experience success by keeping busy and occupied would go a long way to make an unpleasant unemployment experience better.

Summary. The workshops with unemployed people were meant to seek views on: self-perceptions before unemployment; impact of unemployment; leisure activities before and after unemployment; impact on the family; how government and voluntary sectors could help; and how individuals could help themselves.

It was clear that the vast majority of young people (89%) saw themselves as energetic, busy, happy and laidback. Self-perceptions of some were as artistic and sporting people. Employment made them feel good because they were able to set goals and have a purpose in life. It induced healthy social networks and family support.

Unemployment had a gradually adverse impact. It was an unwanted and unpleasant experience characterised by shock, anger and frustration. Many saw themselves as victims. The outcomes of job loss were boredom, depression and low levels of motivation. It was no surprise then, that large proportions of responses reflected low self-esteem and confidence. A very small number (5%) accepted job loss.

Family perceptions compounded feelings of depression, as participants were seen as misfits, expected to look for work, expected to do more jobs in the home and were compared to siblings who may be models to imitate if in employment and not to be like if unemployed. The consistency of feelings of aversion, both real and imagined, fuelled arguments over trivial matters and guilt doing an enjoyable activity.

Participants were involved in a wide array of activities before unemployment. Besides television viewing which was almost universal, team sports, individual activities, social activities and music arts and reading were often mentioned. Leisure activities produced 423 responses resulting in an average of 6.8 activities per person, consistent with a standard for Australian young people.

Job loss had a distinct impact on leisure behaviour. Material and psychological deprivations of unemployment caused increased television viewing, less participation in active sports, more low cost and home-based activities, more time in bed and longer time taken doing tasks. Both increase and decrease were reported by some in smoking and drinking –

increases to alleviate frustrations and decreases because of the lack of money. For some job loss meant more time with friends.

How others – governments and voluntary associations – could help was by way of supply of information, access to leisure and training and being involved in volunteer activity. Participants wanted information about activities that were available and cheaper. They hoped that activities that they were used to – bands and concerts – could be sponsored by public authorities at cheaper rates. Access to leisure could be facilitated by offering concessions and labour training agencies advertising and sponsoring participation.

Young unemployed people showed a generally responsible attitude to how they could help themselves. Getting a job was the prime goal and other solutions were steps which complemented the acquisition of a job, such as attending training sessions, setting personal goals, mixing with others and keeping busy.

5

Unemployment through Lifestyle Interviews

This chapter examines the impact of unemployment on the self, family and leisure of young people in Western Australia. Original quantitative and qualitative data are used to compare the effects of job loss in and out of the home. Before and after job loss comparisons are made to show whether young people's relationships with the family and leisure are diminished in quantity and quality. Similarities and differences in how young males and females cope with unemployment are also discussed.

Impact on Self

When young people were asked what the impact of unemployment was on them, there were two almost equal contrasting responses. The first was one of depression, anger and bitterness, and the second a positive outlook with some sense of relief. Frequencies are in Table 5.1.

There were several reasons given for being angry, bitter and depressed. These included: lack of personal direction;

loyalty counts for nothing; poor timing; hassles with the job; and being angry with the boss.

Table 5.1
Impact of Unemployment

Unemployment Impact	Frequency	Percent
Depressed Angry Bitter	42	51
Positive Outlook - Relief	40	49
Total	82	100.0

The reasons for being positive were varied: excessive overtime; ability to travel now; opportunity to study further; no need to deal with a difficult boss; hope of another job; and a full-time job around the corner.

Aaron, aged 19, thought he lacked personal direction:

> I was pretty messed up. I didn't know where I was going. I was angry with people who were questioning me. I was angry with myself for making my parents upset and for moving away in my decision to do an apprenticeship in boatbuilding rather than motor vehicle building.

For Ailsa, aged 22, loyalty counted for nothing:

> I tried very hard to keep everyone happy. To keep the office environment to the maximum standards because I always did a little bit of work at home. I kept my standard pretty high and I was upset when I lost my job.

Arnold, aged 21, thought losing his job was not his fault:

> I was very angry with everything. I thought it wasn't my own fault. I was doing everything right, but things were going wrong. I was depressed.

On a more purposeful note, Brian, aged 18, wanted to study further:

> I didn't care much, because I would have to go to school to get a better job.

Mark, aged 20, saw no need to put up with a difficult boss:

> I was unhappy. I wasn't getting on with one of my bosses. He was giving me a tough job. So I thought I would get a better job.

Travel was an incentive for Bobby, aged 20, if he did not find another job:

> I had no worries losing a job. Just looked for another job. Will start travelling more.

It was significant that losing their job was not such a significant experience for many young people. Forty-eight percent felt depressed, angry and bitter. The other 52 percent felt relieved and had a positive outlook. This sense of hope is welcomed and the ability to do something about their predicament gave these young people a sense of purpose. The major reasons for being depressed and angry were the lack of direction, loyalty to an employer being wasted, poor timing losing a job, the hassles faced at work (sometimes with the boss) and for reasons other than being competent. Job loss also meant lack of money and frustrations with the job search. These outcomes resulted in depression, anger and bitterness. On the brighter side, the ability to travel, study further, not to have to deal with difficult employers and hope or reemployment, all made the majority of young people feel positive.

Family Relationships

Young people were asked whether their family relationships were affected before and after unemployment. Relationships were categorised as being *good* or *poor*. A *good* relationship was one which was supportive and understanding. A *poor* relationship was characterised by nagging, frequent arguments and disagreements. Each response was categorised on a *good* or *poor* basis. A good-good relationship meant that family members were supportive and understanding before and after unemployment. A good-poor relationship meant that job loss caused family members to make aversive comments and consequently the relationship had changed from what was understanding and supportive to one that was derisive and fractious. Changes in relationships before and after job loss are shown in Table 5.2.

Table 5.2
Family Relationships before and after Unemployment

	Males		Females	
Before/After Unemployment	*Frequency*	*Percent*	*Frequency*	*Percent*
Good-Good	27	55	20	61
Good-Poor	19	39	12	36
Poor-Poor	3	6	1	3
Total	49	100	33	100

Table 5.2 indicates that the family relationships of 39 percent males and 36 percent of females had changed form good to poor. Several reasons were given for the changes: perceived laziness, not trying enough to secure a job, being hassled and nagged, and compared to siblings were common reasons for change of relationships.

Aaron, aged 19, was seen to be lazy and not trying hard enough:

Before: When I had a job, my dad was happy. My parents put pressure on me to get a job, but I didn't really want it. I am usually out of the house all day doing nothing.

After: My family was negative, arguments always came back to me. I was called the lazy bum who stayed at home. Situations got worse and little things started to build up. I reacted aggressively to people and to things. I once put my fist through the door and felt like hitting my parents.

Cameron, aged 19, felt hassled to get a job:

Before: Dinner with family each night, went with family to the beach on weekends. At other times avoided going home because of difficulties with my stepmother.

After: I was hassled to find another job, but family was being helpful, saying that I would feel better with a job. They were negative feelings sitting around all day and eating a lot. I was expected to do more chores and if I didn't it was blamed on visiting friends and arguments started.

Neil, aged 24, spoke of sibling rivalry:

Before: I felt within myself. I felt I was making money and doing myself good sort of thing.

After: Yes, my brothers every time they ring ask if I have a job. They abuse me. They brag and tell me what they are earning compared to what I'm earning, that makes me pretty upset.

Things got so bad for Nola, aged 18, that she often withdrew into her room:

Before: We did things together, we were a pretty happy family.

After: I am not treated well, it's quite different when I had a job. People just lean on me all the time. I have to pay the rent and I can't pay it, so my mum just lays into me like that and dad just joins in. My sister also joins in. I try to be away from the family, I leave the house sometimes, or I just lay in bed and at times I just withdraw into my room.

For Rosemary, aged 25, relationships were very stressful:

Before: Going to the movies, going on picnics, pubs, going dancing, going shopping and buying clothes, restaurants

After: All my relationships became very stressful, I was snappy and hard to get along with and nothing anyone could say would make me feel better.

Among the several good-good relationships was one by Ken, aged 21 who hated not working:

Before: At Port Hedland with the climate and all that, we used to have barbecues on Friday nights and the weekends and have a few laughs. Occasionally I went out with my brothers and sisters. We were a generally happy family.

After: After losing my job I stayed with my family for a while. The relationships were pretty good. I still have some arguments with my sister, but that happened before as well. My mother knew I was out everyday at the CES. They knew I hated not working. I was going mental. I am going mental now. I go door knocking, in the industrial area. Ah, my dad and mum gave me full support.

Pauline, aged 22, was the only female who spoke of a poor-poor relationship:

Before: Nothing really. I have had misfit youth.

After: Big barnies with my mum. She's at me to get a job. I say piss off! I was just depressed as nothing was going to work out. I had a real bad habit, get up at 12 and watch Ricky Lake, see it and go back to bed again. My mum just didn't understand it and my brother would have a go at me. There were negative vibes all round.

One example of a poor-poor relationship was given by Nigel, aged 23:

Before: Basically, I never got along with my family, I do but I hardly talk with them, we do not eat together, if we eat we eat. We will probably eat together on special occasions.

After: Basically, I was put down. How come you haven't got a job, they were negative, mainly nagging and hassling me. Only my mum was supportive, she said don't worry about it, you'll find another job.

The above examples show that the unemployment of young people is a family concern. For many good relationships change to poor. Young people are seen as misfits, lazy and not trying enough to secure paid employment. As noted in the previous chapter they are compared to successful siblings and derided by them as well. Some are left with little option but to withdraw from the others as witnessed in Nola's case.

Activities before Unemployment

Respondents were asked to give the activities they participated in before unemployment in the home, for fitness, sociability, entertainment and in clubs and associations. The means of each category appear in Table 5.3.

Table 5.3
Means of Activities Per Person before Unemployment

Activity	Mean
Home	2.43
Fitness	1.74
Social	1.25
Entertainment	1.06
Clubs & Associations	0.68
Total	7.16

The data indicate that young employed people are highly active in leisure activities in and out of the home. The mean total per person is 7.16 activities. All categories exceed one activity, except for memberships in clubs and associations, which indicates that some in the sample did not belong to a club or association. The mean total for females (7.46) exceeds that for males (6.96), the difference being in home-based activities (for females it was 2.72 and for males, 2.24). There were negligible differences in the means between females and males in fitness, social, entertainment, and club and association categories.

Home-based Recreation

Young people engaged in a wide range of home-based activities before unemployment. Eleven most frequent activities are listed in Table 5.4.

Table 5.4
Leisure at Home before Unemployment

Activity	Frequency	Percent	Rank
Television	72	36	1
Gardening	28	14	2
Reading/writing	22	11	3
Videos	19	9.5	4
Listening to music	16	8	5
Cooking/home/car maintenance	15	7.5	6
Board/Table games	9	4.5	7
Electronic hobbies	8	4	8
Modelling/craft work	5	2.5	9
Swimming (home pool)	4	2	10
Playing musical instrument	2	1	11
No. of responses	200	100.0	
Respondents (N)	82		
Activities per individual = 2.43			

The six most popular home activities were television viewing, gardening, videos, reading/writing, cooking/home/car maintenance, and listening to music. Five other activities ranked lower were board/table games, electronic hobbies, swimming (home pool), playing a musical instrument and modelling and craft work. In order to show whether male and female rankings were similar, Kendall's coefficient of concordance was applied. A correlation of .947 was obtained, which is statistically significant (p=.04), and indicates a high level of agreement between the ranking of home activities between males and females.

Each response on participation in home-based activities was categorised on a before and after unemployment basis. Responses which indicated a substantial amount of time spent on recreation activities in the home were categorised as *high*. Responses which indicated that very little was done in the home, were categorised as *low*. Home-based activity frequencies on a before and after unemployment basis are shown in Table 5.5.

Table 5.5
Home-based Leisure before and after Unemployment

Before/After Unemployment	Frequency	Percent
High-High	55	67
High-Low	15	18
Low-Low	7	9
Low- High	5	6
Total	82	100

The majority (67%) of young people that were *high* on home-based activities before unemployment continued to be *high* after job loss. The proportion of females (73%) was higher than that of males (64%). A substantially lower number (18%) had changed from *high* to *low* and the percentage for male and female was identical. In the *low-low* category, nine percent were uninvolved in home-based leisure before and after job loss, but this was applicable only to males. Six percent had changed from *low* to *high* and this category included two males and three females.

Several reasons were given for high levels of activity in the home after job loss. These included: more time to do things of interest (9 responses); taking on more home roles (6); parents asked them to do chores (4); good to keep busy (3); more help from friends; more independent living; find strategies to do things cheaply (1). Reasons for low levels of activity were: boredom and lack of motivation (9); wanting to be alone; outdoors oriented; lack of money for home interests (2); and ill-health (1). Females tended to be more involved at home than males, though reasons for high and low involvement after job loss are similar for both sexes.

Keeping busy, being bored, and lacking motivation were the major ways of coping with unemployment in the home and adaptation was common to both males and females as the following examples show. Gary aged, 30, kept busy and depended on friends to help his home development:

Before: Watching TV. Plus I own my home. If I didn't own the house, I would be bored. Everything I have put into it is for my benefit. I can maintain it. I did gardening, but not as much, because driving trucks did not give me enough time.

After: I did a lot of things at home. I have a lot of friends. They came to my home and dug my fish pond and things like that. My mate brought a trailer, they do all the hard work instead of me doing it.

Rosemary, aged 25, was bored and spent much time 'just sitting around' around after unemployment:

Before: Watching TV, enjoyed playing scrabble, listening to music and generally chatting to my family writing letters to friends.

After: I spent a lot more time at home, sleeping and watching more TV, may be just going for a walk in the park so that I could just get out of the house. I spent a lot of time just sitting around.

Steve, aged 26, did similar activities before and after unemployment, but they had a different meaning:

Before: Mechanical work, that's my activities. I worked in the shed, repairing the car, panel beating. It was my recreation. I watched some TV.

After: I watch TV, just go out to do some work in the shed, the garden. Now I am here on this stupid course. When I am not, I just sit there and watch TV. Sometimes I can't afford to go out. Have to wait till next dole day.

Young people tend to engage in a range of home-based activities prior to unemployment. Males and females participate in similar activities. The level of home-based activities before and after unemployment tended to be high for more than two-thirds of the sample. It could therefore be inferred that the quantity of home-based activities for the majority was not diminished after job loss. However, concern must be expressed for the 18 percent of both sexes whose levels of home activities was lower than before unemployment.

There was evidence that the quality of leisure at home was diminished across the sample, even among those who continued to be active after job loss. There were those who had more time to do things of interest, to take more home roles, to do chores at parents' requests and to keep busy. In Steve's account above, recreation activities in employment had a different meaning after job loss. Ailsa, aged 22, took on more home roles of reading and cooking, in addition to gardening and watching television, activities she did before unemployment. Likewise, George, aged 21, "did a lot more housework" in addition to his pre-unemployment activities. In his case, as in Ailsa's and Steve's they wanted to keep busy and to fill time. Their accounts were repeated over and over again by many of the other subjects.

There must be concern for those who changed from high to low home involvement after job loss. Boredom and lack of motivation were by far the major reasons for participating in fewer home-based activities. Thus much time was spent passively, watching television, sleeping or "just sitting around". Earlier data on the impact of unemployment on these young people revealed that those who were severely affected had much difficulty in coping with enforced unobligated time brought by job loss. This finding is consistent with that of older unemployed people who were passive in their leisure at home after being adversely and severely affected by job loss. Despite possessing and utilising their leisure skills while in employment, they could not motivate themselves to participate in recreation activities which they were formerly accustomed to (Lobo, 1998).

It may be concluded that for the majority of young people, two-thirds of the sample, the *quantity* of home-based leisure after unemployment was the same or had increased. For 18 percent, the quantity of leisure activities in the home was reduced. A very small proportion (6%) who were low changed to high, simply because they had returned home after staying away from home during employment. Across the sample, the *quality* of leisure in the home was reduced. It was mainly used to fill time by keeping busy. For those who were severely affected by job loss, the quantity of home-based leisure was not only diminished, but the quality of leisure was reduced to passivity by the lack of motivation and boredom.

Out-of-Home Recreation for Fitness

Young people were asked to name the activities they participated in for fitness before unemployment. The activities included organised sport, walking, gym/aerobics, bike riding, surfing/skiing, swimming, jogging, golf, and tennis (Table 5.6).

Application of the Kendall's correlation of concordance to rankings of males and females resulted in a coefficient of .696 which was statistically insignificant (p=.194), but showed moderate agreement. Organised sport was ranked first with both sexes, with males showing 12 percent higher involvement. Gym/aerobics on the other hand, ranked 2 by females and 6 by males showed a 15.4 percent difference in favour of females. The mean of activities per individual was 1.74 with negligible gender difference. (for males 1.73 and for females 1.75).

Table 5.6
Fitness Activities before Unemployment

Activity	Frequency	Percent	Rank
Organised sport	62	43.3	1
Walking	21	14.7	2
Gym/aerobics	19	13.3	3
Bike riding	10	7.0	4
Surfing/skiing	9	6.3	5
Swimming	8	5.6	6
Jogging	6	4.2	7
Golf	5	3.5	8
Tennis	3	2.1	9
No. of responses	143	100.0	
Respondents (N)	82		
Activities per individual = 1.74			

Activities for fitness during employment and after job loss were categorised on a before and after basis. Those who participated regularly were classified as *active*. Those who gave a "no" response or said they did nothing were classified as *passive*. Before and after job loss comparisons on frequencies and percentages are shown in Table 5.7.

Table 5.7
Fitness Activities before and after Unemployment

Before/After Unemployment	Frequency	Percent
Active-Active	41	50
Active- Passive	35	43
Passive-Passive	6	7
Total	82	100.0

The data in Table 5.7 reveal that 50 percent of young people in the study (males 51%; females 49%) maintained active lifestyles before and after job loss. However, a substantial proportion of 43 percent (males 41%; females 45%) who were passive after job loss having been active before unemployment. There were several reasons for passivity, but the major reason was the inability to afford participation in an activity. Thirty-eight respondents stated that they could not afford participation, this included 20 males and 18 females. Passivity was also induced by depression and the lack of motivation for four males and two females. Injury caused three to be inactive and not being a sporting person (1) and lack of transport (1) were also stated. Reasons for being active were: to release anger and frustration (7 all males); more time for fitness (13 - male 6; female 7); and continuation of activity because of low cost (4 - male 3; female 1).

Some examples of how young people's fitness was affected include: having more time for fitness; being depressed; and problems of having less money. Abel, aged 18, found more time to surf and keep fitter.

> *Before*: Surfing every weekend 6.00 am to 5.00 pm; If the surf was not good, went bike riding; During the week played indoor cricket with the work team.

> *After*: Surfing much more, all day everyday if possible. My motor bike blew up, so I couldn't use it. Cricket ceased, but I have just started water polo in the last two weeks.

Arthur, aged 28 was so depressed, that he ceased swimming and playing his sport:

> *Before*: I played football with my mates at the local oval daily. I also went swimming with my girlfriend two or three times a week.

> *After*: I stopped playing footy. I was depressed and felt a lesser person than my mates. So I didn't join them. I also broke up with my girl friend, so I didn't go swimming.

Kathy, aged 24, says how employment enhances fitness and lack of money constrains participation.

Before: Touch rugby, tennis, swimming, hockey surf life saving.

After: Fitness goes hand in hand with employment, because once you have a routine in employment you go out and join clubs. When you're unemployed you are sitting around and hunting for jobs. So while I am travelling and looking for a job, tennis and the other things I would be doing is reduced. I am less active, but money has a restriction on the things I can and cannot do.

Comment: Young people participated in large numbers in organised sport. Except for golf, which only males in the sample participated in, all other activities were common to both sexes. The ranking of activities for a correlation of concordance between males and females was statistically insignificant, but showed moderate levels of agreement. The data show that 50 percent of young people in the study remained active after unemployment. The reasons stated for continued activity were: more time for fitness (6 males; 7 females); to release anger and frustration (7 males); and low cost of participating in the activity (3 males; 1 female).

The major reason for passivity after unemployment was because as many as 38 respondents could not afford to participate in the activity. Inability to afford participation applied equally to males and females. However, there were those who were depressed and unmotivated and that number included four males and two females. The data clearly show that half of the sample, discontinued their fitness activities after job loss, and this was due, as Kathy stated, to the lack of money and the normal routine of employment being broken as young people sat around and spent time looking for jobs.

It can be concluded that job loss diminished the quantity of fitness activities for half of the young people in the study. By not engaging in these activities, the quality of leisure was reduced. Material deprivation, namely, the lack of money was the major cause of non-participation in fitness activities, but to a lesser extent, depression and the ensuing lack of motivation to participate, contributed to passivity. It must be noted that there were three significant reasons why some people continued with fitness activities. There were six males and seven females that used time imposed by unemployment to improve their fitness. The anger and frustration as a result of job loss caused seven males to continue with fitness activities. For three males and one female, low cost of the fitness activity enabled them to continue with it.

Out-of-Home Recreation for Sociability

When asked to give details of their out-of-home recreation for sociability, common responses included: visiting friends and family; pubs parties and dinners; and picnics and barbecues. As shown in Table 5.8, visiting family and friends was by far the most popular social activity (56%), with higher rates for males (61%) than females (50.0%). High rates were also noted for pubs, parties and dinners (35%), with males (33%) lower than females (38%). Very small proportions (9%) went for picnics and barbecues - males (7%) and females (12%). The mean score for social activities per individual was 1.25, with very little difference between males (1.24) and females (1.27).

Table 5.8
Social Activities before Unemployment

Activity	Frequency	Percent
Visiting friends and relatives	58	56
Picnics and barbecues	9	9
Pubs, parties and dinners	36	35
No. of responses	103	100
Respondents (N)	82	
Activities per individual = 1.25		

Before and after unemployment comparisons were made on the basis of being *involved* and *uninvolved*. Those who visited friends and relatives regularly were categorised as *involved*. Those who let their friends drop off or who did not mix with others, were categorised as *uninvolved*. Before and after responses are presented in Table 5.9.

A high proportion (51%) of young people (males 49%; females 55%) who were involved before unemployment became uninvolved after job loss. High, but lesser proportions (41.5%) of young people (males 41%; females 42%) continued being involved after unemployment. Two people (one male and one female) who were uninvolved before became involved after, because they lived away from home during their working life, but returned home after losing their job.

Table 5.9
Social Activities before and after Unemployment

Before/After Unemployment	Frequency	Percent
Involved-Involved	34	41.5
Involved-Uninvolved	42	51
Uninvolved-Uninvolved	4	5
Uninvolved-Involved	2	2.5
Total	82	100.0

Ten responses indicate that the main reason for being involved with friends was because they had more time to visit and mix with them. Five females still mixed with friends, not in the pub as formerly, but in homes. There were cases of males who mixed with their unemployed mates, or with the same sports group before job loss, or because meeting friends was cheaper than going to the movies. Twenty-five people, 15 male and 10 female, gave the lack of money as the reason for not socialising with friends. Depression and social discomfort were also cited as reasons for not mixing with others. Four people said that former friends were those at work and did not live in their neighbourhood, which resulted in reduced socialising. There were some examples of less social mixing, less social reciprocity, less money and reduced frequency of drinks in pubs, and envy of employment.

Jane, aged 27, was fond of mixing with others before unemployment, but felt too depressed to be in their company after job loss:

> *Before*: I had friends and generally they were connected to people at work and friends of people I worked with. We would go out to a club in the weekends, sometimes maybe camping, a movie maybe, things that cost money.

> *After*: I didn't mix with others. I just wanted to stay home and didn't want to mix with others at all.

Ken, aged 21, had problems reciprocating his friends' hospitality, so he went less often to the pub:

> *Before*: When I was working I used to have a few cans of beer with my mates and grab a steak and have whatever is around with not a care in the world. I went camping, fishing, motor bike riding, working on cars, went to the pub, with a few friends.

> *After*: After a while I did not go out to the pub with my friends, many of them tradesmen. They used to say "don't worry about cash, come on" but I couldn't do that everyday without giving a shout. Certainly, being social slowed down a lot. Instead of going two or three times a week, I went once a week.

Peter, aged 29, still went to the pub, but had fewer drinks:

> *Before*: I did a bit of fishing, mixed with my friends, went to the pub.

> *After*: I still go to the pub once a week, but I have fewer drinks.

Thelma, aged 19, felt uncomfortable with her employed friends, but was more at home with those who were unemployed:

Before: I went for social outings. I used to go out for drinks. Then I'd go to the movies, to the theatre or something.

After: I was a bit offish with my friends, because they've got a job and I haven't. You feel really uncomfortable because they have the money and you're sitting back without a job. I was more comfortable with my unemployed friends, because they share things with you, they don't fob you off sort of thing.

Young people were generally socially active before unemployment. Large numbers visited friends and relatives, attended parties and dinners, and frequented pubs. They socialised to a lesser extent at picnics and barbecues. After job loss, social activity was adversely affected for many in the study. There were several reasons for this. More than half the sample indicated that their social activities were reduced in employment.

Lack of money was the major cause. This was stated by both males (15) and females (10). All complained about the lack of money; Jane could not go camping, Ken could not reciprocate his friends' hospitality and Peter had fewer drinks at the pub.

Lack of money, coupled with social discomfort in the company of employed friends, also caused some to reduce social mixing. Thelma felt uncomfortable with her employed friends because they had the money and she did not. She was more comfortable with her unemployed friends because they were more understanding. Thelma's social network was therefore affected and limited to unemployed friends. The confining of social networks of the unemployed has been noted by Gallie et. al (1995), but there is also another situation where the only friends of the unemployed may have been in the work environment and not living in the neighbourhood. Thus unemployment causes loss of contact with former friends. There were at least three cases (2 female, 1 male) where depression caused by job loss led to social isolation.

Nine people said that unemployment resulted in spending more time with friends. Females generally continued contact with their friends but it was usually in homes, rather than at the pub where they used to meet during employment days.

It may be concluded that the social involvement of young people tends to be adversely affected as a result of job loss. It is affected quantitatively and qualitatively. Young people tend not to cease visiting the pub, but the frequency of visits or the number of drinks purchased may be reduced because of the lack of money. Qualitatively, social leisure is diminished as social networks are restricted or job loss results in self-imposed isolation.

Out-of-Home Recreation for Entertainment

Young people were asked about the types of entertainment they participated while they were employed. The activities, frequencies and percentages are given in Table 5.10.

Table 5.10
Entertainment Activities before Unemployment

Activity	Frequency	Percent
Movies/Cinema	44	51
Night clubs/discos	23	26
Bands/concerts	11	13
Arcades and pool parlours	9	10
No. of responses	87	100.0
Respondents (N)	82	
Activities per individual = 1.06		

Before unemployment young people went to movies and the cinema very frequently and high levels of attendance were noted for night clubs and discos. Both sexes ranked movies and cinema (51%) ahead of night clubs and discos (26.5%). There were lesser frequencies for bands and concerts (13%) and visiting arcades and pool parlours (10%). The mean number of entertainment activities per individual was 1.06.

Before and after comparisons were made on a *frequent* and *infrequent* basis. Those who said they attended some form of entertainment regularly or once a month were categorised as *frequent*. Those who used words like "rarely" or "occasionally" or "not at all" were categorised as *infrequent*. The before and after responses are in Table 5.11.

Table 5.11
Entertainment Activities before and after Unemployment

Before/After Unemployment	Frequency	Percent
Frequent/Infrequent	48	58
Frequent/Frequent	17	21
Infrequent/Infrequent	13	16
Infrequent/Frequent	2	2.5
Unclear response	2	2.5
Total	82	100.0

Unemployment affected the entertainment of 58% of young people in the study. There were a higher number of females (70%) than males (51%). Twenty-one percent of all young people continued to attend entertainment activities after unemployment, males (25%) more than females (15%). The reasons for frequent entertainment after unemployment were: possession of equipment by males (4); cheaper entertainment (males 3; females 4); more time for entertainment (males 2); still go to night clubs but don't drink much (male 1, female 1). Forty responses (male 23, female 17) indicated lack of finance, five lack of motivation (males 3; females 2) and one male felt that the entertainment available was not appealing.

Examples of adapting to less entertainment after job loss were doing things cheaply, using assets in possession, doing less with less and withdrawing socially. Ailsa, aged 22, became more responsible and did things cheaply:

Before: I went quite a bit to discos, driving, dinner quite a lot once or twice a week.

After: Yes, that suffered going to discos and that. It made me grow mentally to take more responsibility of the money side. I couldn't afford it. We did it cheaply, more picnics, more barbecues, go for a bike ride with my brothers, sightseeing, display homes.

Arnold, aged 21, used his musical instruments to keep occupied with rehearsals with his mates:

Before: Went with my girlfriend to the swimming pool, bands, movies usually once a week and sometimes three times a week.

After: I sat at home and listened to music. Played in a band with mates in an organised group and rehearsed in a studio in the city. Hung around pubs, drinking.

Brian, aged 21, just did less with because money was tight:

Before: Went to the computer arcade, night clubs every weekend, movies once a week and computer games, pool parlours, pot black.

After: I went to my friends home for computer games but not the arcade. I went out less because money was tight.

Tess, aged 27, just withdrew socially:

Before: Movies, I used to go out and see a band.

After: I don't go to the movies any more, I don't go out socially, because I can't afford it. I last went to a movie about five months ago because a friend took me and paid for it.

Young people patronised the entertainment industry in large numbers before unemployment, particularly going to movies and night clubs. They also attended bands and concerts – males more than females – and to a lesser extent pool parlours. Lack of income seriously affected participation in entertainment for most unemployed young people. But both males and females were able to adapt by entertaining themselves with items of equipment they already possessed, substituting cheaper activity, doing less with less, and for some who lacked motivation and were financially deprived by doing without any entertainment. There was little difference in the various adaptation responses between males and females.

Membership in Clubs and Associations

Membership in clubs and associations was the fifth category of the leisure experience of young people. They were asked whether or not they were members of clubs and associations. Of the 82 participants in the study, 47 were members of clubs and associations. Membership frequencies and percentages before unemployment are in Table 5.12.

Table 5.12
Memberships in Clubs and Associations before Unemployment

Before Unemployment	Frequency	Percent
Membership	47	57
No Membership	35	43
Total	82	100.0

Before unemployment, young people belonged to sporting (59%), special interest (18%), social (16%) and service (7%) clubs and associations. Some people had memberships in more than one club or association. Therefore, the total number of responses exceeded the number of respondents. The mean total of club and association membership per individual was 0.68. Frequencies and percentages of membership in clubs and associations are in Table 5.13.

The responses of members in clubs and associations were categorised on a *"retained"* and *"discontinued"* basis. If membership was continued after job loss, the response was classified as being *retained*. If membership lapsed or was

Table 5.13
Club and Association Membership before Unemployment

Activity	Frequency	Percent
Sporting	33	59
Special Interest	10	18
Social	9	16
Service	4	7
No. of responses	56	100.0
Respondents (N)	47	
Activities per individual = 0.68		

terminated, the response was classified as *discontinued*. The frequencies of *retained* and *discontinued* membership in clubs and associations are in Table 5.14.

Table 5.14
Club and Association Membership before and after
Unemployment

Before/After Unemployment	Frequency	Percent
Retained-Retained	22	47
Retained-Discontinued	25	53
	47	100.0

Forty-seven percent of those who were members of clubs and associations retained membership after job loss. Fifty-three percent discontinued membership. Three reasons were given for the retaining membership. Seven young people (5 males, 2 females) had already paid their memberships. Eleven (males 7, females 4) found the membership low cost and cheap. Two (male 1, female 1) were voluntary members of special interest associations, which had no membership fee.

The major reason for the discontinuation of membership was lack of finance. Fourteen young people, seven males and seven females, said that they could not afford membership fees.

Lack of motivation was also given by five respondents (males 4, females 1). Two other reasons for discontinuing membership were a change in residence and injury. The following are illustrations of why some young people chose to discontinue and why others retained membership.

Cameron, aged 19, attended a recreation centre regularly, but had to pay a separate fee for the use of the gymnasium. He had this to say:

Before: Lakes Recreation Centre, pool, basketball, gym twice a week.

After: Gym membership lapsed as I had no money.

Alison, aged 29, was a member of a gymnasium. When she lost her job, she could not afford the subscription, so her mother helped out.

Before: Only gym membership.

After: I still go to the gym. I got a nice mum at home who pays for it.

Kay, aged 22, was a member of a sports club, which was low cost. She saw no reason to discontinue her membership.

Before: I was a member of the softball club.

After: I am still a member of the softball club, but that hasn't changed. It doesn't cost a lot of money. It's the same as when you play, you don't pay membership.

Austin, aged 21, found that his club was close to home, as well as low cost. So he retained his membership.

Before: I am a member of the computer club and part of the social club playing lawn bowls.

After: Not really, I still play lawn bowls, the club is close to the house, in walking distance and fees are only about 5 dollars. If the club was a long way away, it would definitely affect it, because getting there would be impossible.

Of the 82 young people in the study, 47 belonged to clubs and associations during employment. After unemployment, more than half (25 people) discontinued their memberships in clubs and associations. Three reasons were given for retaining membership. Many had already paid their annual dues when they lost their job, so their memberships were still current. Others found since their subscriptions were cheap or low cost they could afford not to terminate their memberships. Participation in special interest associations was voluntary and did not have a membership fee, so the two people saw no reason to discontinue membership.

The majority of young people who decided to discontinue membership did so because they lacked finance to pay for it. This applied equally to males and females. The psychological impact of unemployment caused at least five young people to discontinue their membership. As in other aspects of their leisure, they did not have the motivation to participate in activities offered by clubs and associations.

It may be concluded that job loss causes many young people to cease membership in clubs and associations. The major reason is lack of finance to pay membership fees. In a small number of cases, the psychological impact of unemployment affects individuals so severely that the self-imposed isolation triggers them to leave clubs and associations.

Conclusions

This chapter examined the impact of unemployment on the self, family and leisure of young people in Western Australia. It sought to find out whether leisure in the home, for fitness, sociability, entertainment and in clubs and associations diminished as a result of unemployment.

The impact of unemployment on the self was more or less evenly divided between being depressed, angry and bitter on the one hand and being positive and relieved on the other. Reasons for depression and anger were the lack of personal direction, misplaced loyalty to an employer, hassles at work and conditions beyond one's control. The positive outlook was the opportunity to study further, travel, not having to deal with a difficult boss and the hope of reemployment.

The unemployment of young people is a family concern. For many good relationships change to poor. Young people are seen as misfits, lazy and not trying enough to secure paid employment. As noted in the previous chapter they are compared to successful siblings and derided by them as well. Some are left with little option but to physically withdraw from others.

It was found that for the majority of young people the quantity of home-based leisure after unemployment was the same or had increased. For a small proportion, which included those who were psychologically adversely affected, the quantity of leisure activities was reduced. Many young people were active in the home and kept busy in order to fill the large blocks of unobligated time which unemployment imposes on individuals. The leisure of those severely affected by job loss was reduced to passivity as a consequence of a lack of motivation and apparent boredom.

Organised sport was very much in the repertoire of young people's leisure for fitness before unemployment. Fifty percent of young people continued to be active after job loss and the quantity of their leisure did not diminish. For the other half it did. The major reasons for continuing with fitness activities were because more time was available to pursue fitness activities, some were able to release their anger and frustration, and a few found the cost of participation low enough for them to continue. The other half who had ceased participation not only diminished the quantity of fitness activities, but by disengaging reduced the quality of their leisure experience. The major reason for the discontinuation of many fitness activities was lack of money, which was felt by both males and females.

The social involvement of young people was adversely affected by job loss quantitatively and qualitatively. Lack of money was again cited for reduced social engagement with friends at venues such as pubs. Qualitatively, it was found that social networks were restricted to other unemployed friends who were in the same boat and who had mutual understanding of the deprivations of job loss. In some cases, social discomfort in the company of others led to self-imposed isolation.

Entertainment was seriously affected quantitatively by the lack of money. Without certain forms of entertainment, it could be inferred that the quality of the social and leisure world of the individual was diminished. However, getting involved in cheaper forms of entertainment and doing less with less showed favourable signs of adaptation by young people.

Continuation of membership in clubs and associations was seriously affected by job loss. Unemployment caused large numbers to cease membership because of the lack of finance. Material deprivation not only caused a diminution of leisure quantitatively, but also affected the individual's overall leisure qualitatively. Those severely affected by unemployment chose to isolate themselves, but that isolation was also complemented by lack of money to continue membership.

The overall conclusions to the questions raised in this chapter are that many young people are devastated by unemployment, but as many see job loss as a relief. In several cases, family relationships deteriorated as a result. Except for home-based activities, unemployment tends to reduce the quantity of leisure activities out of the home. Material and psychological deprivation jointly impact on the individual to reduce the quality of the many leisure activities that young people engage in, including those in the home. These findings may not apply universally but the general trend is that unemployment does diminish the quantity and quality of leisure of young people.

6

Effects of Unemployment on Categories of Experience

This chapter deals with depth interviews with ten females and ten males. The interviews focus on eight categories of the unemployment experience. They are: unemployment impact; job search; reduced income; family relationships and responsibilities; activities in the home; activities out of home; personal resources; and external resources. The responses of the young people are reported in abbreviated form touching on each of categories of experience during unemployment. The reports are written incorporating the language used by the unemployed young females and males. In order to make comparisons between individuals in each cohort group, a there is a table which summarises qualitative data in cells on each of the categories of experience. Finally the effects of each of the categories of experience are discussed in terms of similarities and differences. Pseudonyms are used to protect the identity of the participants.

Females

Lesley, aged 19

Lesley worked as a check-out operator when she lost her job. She distinguished between getting paid for a job and unemployment benefits:

> It was long days standing on my feet but I was upset only because I had lost the feeling of security of having a job. It made me feel good to know that I could go somewhere everyday and I'd get paid for it, whereas on unemployment benefits they stuff your pay up and some weeks you don't get paid because you've done something wrong or something like that. It really frustrates you being on the dole.

Immediately after losing her job, Lesley felt depressed, but being pregnant relieved some of the stress. She was on a pension, sat at home all day and was bored. After her daughter was born, looking after the baby was a trying experience. Not having transport, confined her to the home. Three months prior to the interview Lesley felt suicidal and was admitted to hospital, where she stayed for three days for psychological assessment. At the time of the interview, she had a much more positive attitude to life in general and in her words was "doing everything to get a job".

Joining a Job Club made her feel better, because she had learnt computer skills. She was trying hard to get a job. On the previous Monday, she made telephone calls to more than thirty different businesses. The next day she sent off approximately fifteen letters to companies with her resumé. A day later, she had a job interview, but missed out due to lack of experience. On Friday she didn't do much, but in an earlier week she made phone calls, sent letters and a fax. She had approached the Commonwealth Employment Services (CES) several times in the week and applied for four or five jobs. Frustrations in getting a job were the lack of transport and the use of appropriate clothing to enhance her personal appearance. She had to catch a bus or a train to wherever she had to go, which limited her range of job search. Lack of experience and qualifications were reasons given for rejection by employers and she hoped that employers "went out on a limb for me so I could get some experience and some training". Having a young daughter and trying to get a job with little family support were frustrating.

As a single parent she had State subsidized housing, which was some distance away from where her separated parents lived. Her father lived fifteen kilometres away and her mother fifty. She got on well with her father and visited him once or twice a week. The relationship with her mother was not as good, and being further away she visited her once in two months or on special occasions like birthdays. The baby's father abandoned Lesley, so she did "pretty much everything" by herself. Her boyfriend had moved in and he gave some help that Lesley appreciated. She felt badly about receiving a pension, while her sisters and brother were in paid employment and she was just "sitting at home looking after a child wondering when I am going to get a job...Yeah, it was just a really, really hard time".

Reduced income forced Lesley to buy second hand clothes, go to cheaper supermarkets, take her daughter out less, buy fewer toys than other mums, and pay bills by instalments. This state of affairs was very different from when she was employed and would think nothing of buying a $20 top and paying bills promptly.

Besides minding her daughter at home, which limited much of what Lesley could do at home, she played electronic games and owned a play station and Nintendo. She hired games, played darts and did something in the garden. This form of entertainment replaced going out to dinners, which were regular events when she was employed. Drinking at home was reduced, as was having friends over for dinner.

Lesley, her daughter and boyfriend went out, but could only afford cheaper forms of recreation:

> Yeah, we go to parks and take my daughter there. She loves that. We go and sit down and have fish and chips on the jetty. So, yes, we do things like that. Just to make sure we do that once a week.

Lesley perceived herself as a very independent person and deliberately kept herself occupied doing house work and playing with the baby – "typically everyday stuff that other people take for granted...(which she) was really enjoying". At the time of the interview she felt positive and was very enthusiastic about getting paid employment.

Family and friends gave Lesley good emotional support, in particular her father and boyfriend. She spoke well of the CES and Skillshare. Collectively, family, friends and other external supports assisted greatly in restoring Lesley's rapidly decreasing self-esteem which resulted from losing her job and subsequent rejection of job applications.

Marion, aged 23

Marion reported being 'demoralized' and 'depressed' when she was unemployed. She remembered the depression 'just hitting her' and she felt lost and at the end of her tether.

Marion's parents were not particularly supportive during her unemployment. They pointed out the difficulties of finding jobs and how important it was to start as soon as possible. This added to Marion's feelings of unhappiness. Immediately after she lost her job she lacked energy and motivation to begin the job search. She reported simply 'cruising around from day-to-day wondering what she was going to do'. She often lacked the motivation to get out of bed to and sustaining motivation was a very real problem.

When asked what steps she had taken to find work Marion replied 'none'. She was interviewed at a local Job

Club, but had been referred there by a CES office and was going there in order not to have her unemployment allowance affected by refusing to attend. Marion said that soon after losing her job she actively sought work by making telephone calls and sending out her resumé. She felt initially confident "having five months experience as a trainee executive assistant". After several rejection letters she felt 'kicked in the guts' and realised that her experience counted for little and the chance of obtaining a position in the area was remote. Marion abandoned trying to find work about one month after losing her job, saying her motivation was gone and her 'depression' – coupled with the frustrations of job searching – had led her to conclude that her efforts would amount to nothing so 'why try?'

Marion talked about a series of frustrations in the search for work. Her qualifications were "not enough". She believed her age contributed to not being successful. Marion was too young to have accumulated the amount of experience prospective employers seemed to require: "They (employers) expect ten pages of a resumé, you know, completely full of all this experience and everything. It's something you just don't get these days'. She felt upset that she was in a 'catch-22' situation, did not have the experience to get the position, but could not initially obtain a position to gain experience.

Marion's reduced income also contributed to her frustrations and motivation to seek employment. She said she had clothes for interviews, but everyday living was difficult. Running her car was costly and taking public transport to job interviews was difficult. By the time she arrived she felt tired and not at her best (possibly contributing to why she believed she was not successful in obtaining the position). When money became constantly tight she began not "being bothered to get out of bed in the morning". Lack of money "demoralised" her. She reported that there was always 'so much to be done' (with money) that she had great difficulty making it stretch. There was rent to her parents, car expenses, and general bills to pay. Marion reported that her parents would occasionally allow her to skip rent if she had a good reason for doing so. Her mother would do the shopping and pay the bills.

Even though money was a problem Marion said she was "still going out as much", but limiting her budget by only taking a set amount (usually $20) to night clubs. She would also time her entry into the clubs during the free entry periods. Marion would not 'drive around as much' looking for entertainment venues as much as she did when she was employed due to the cost of petrol. She reports still doing all the things she used to do before job loss for entertainment, but spending less on them.

Marion believed that losing her job had an impact upon the household. There was a degree of "anxiety" about her situation. Her parents would constantly comment that she was not trying hard enough to obtain work, they often threatened to turn Marion out of the family home if she did not try harder. It caused Marion to 'steer clear' of her parents by keeping different hours to them, staying up late and sleeping in. She considered that her unemployment had a 'very' negative effect upon the whole family.

Marion tended to spend longer periods in the home. She watched more television, used the phone more, used the computer more and watched more videos. This change in her leisure patterns resulted in increased power bills and more friction between family members. She engaged in 'kill time' activities such as house cleaning, but stopped after a time due to feeling she was not getting any recognition from her father that she was contributing.

Her out-of-home leisure was also negatively affected beyond the fact she simply had less money. She reported 'not being herself' when she went out with friends. Marion felt this 'brought her friends down to her level' when she was out with them and so would often decline their invitations out. Her sporting commitments also ceased because she was not able to afford the fees.

Marion said that her friends would be a better judge of her inner strengths and traits. She said: "You just have to be persistent. You've just got to keep an outlook on life. You've just got to think there is something out there for me. I've got to find it and I'll do it". As for external resources she reported not "using family or friends for that". Once again, she felt it was better not to involve them too heavily in her problems as it had a negative effect on them. Marion appreciated that her friends and family were there and that they were supportive, but seemed to not want to utilise them as a support. She did not mention other agencies, such as the Job Club as external supports.

Marion reported losing her job and subsequently searching for other jobs was emotionally difficult. Her self-esteem was 'down the drain', there had been an impact on family and friends and 'depression' was a continuing issue.

Deborah, aged 21

Deborah lost her last position due to a reduction in her working hours. Her understanding was that her employer wanted her to leave and so reduced her hours to such an extent she 'could not live on them' so had to leave. Deborah felt disappointed and let down that they would not actually sack her and allow her to obtain unemployment benefits. She has been out of work for two years since losing that position.

Losing her job had an immediate impact on Deborah. She was living away from the family home and not having employment put her in a difficult financial situation. She reported not having enough money 'to cope with everyday things'. Unemployment immediately affected Deborah's ability to socialise, to 'get out and do something different instead of sitting around doing the same old thing'. She missed the structure a job provided, having to be somewhere at a certain time. The longer she was without employment the more 'down' she became.

Being referred to the Job club has resulted in Deborah obtaining a trainee position in a restaurant. Previous to this she reported writing letters to potential employers, making phone calls and looking in newspapers for positions. Deborah felt very frustrated and 'let down' by this process. One particular frustration was not receiving any replies from prospective employers she had contacted. This lack of replying impacted upon her self-esteem, making her feel worthless. Other frustrations caused by reduced income included not being able to buy new clothes for interviews, the cost of petrol to attend interviews and general living expenses. She reported initially not seeking work as actively as she had recently. Initially she did not contemplate that finding a position would be too difficult, but as time progressed she became aware that it would be more difficult than she had assumed.

Deborah survived on a reduced income spending money on necessities (food, electricity and petrol) and not 'going out'. She said she had not been out for 'two or three months' at the time of the interview. Deborah would go to parties because they were cheaper than pubs, nightclubs etc. She said her 'whole lifestyle has changed' as far as entertainment away from home is concerned. She does not see friends as often because she feels unable to go with the to these venues. Shopping included buying predominantly black and gold brand items as well as taking note of advertised prices in catalogues in order to buy the cheapest meat etc.

A reduced income meant that Deborah had to occasionally borrow money from her father. This caused some family friction. There was also the added difficulty of being home more often and her father 'having enough of me mopping around'. Deborah reported doing more leisure activities at home, playing on the computer, more television. She drank at home as a leisure activity. This became a problem as she 'drank more than I should have'. It was at this stage she identified depression as an issue. Deborah complained that 'everyone sort of turned their backs on me when I started drinking'.

When she recognized this was becoming a problem she pulled her self out of it with the help of her father. Losing her job had made her depressed and she had begun to drink as a way of dealing with the situation.

Deborah's out-of-home activities suffered. She could no longer afford to play netball and had to give it up. The cost of transport, equipment and ancillary costs became too expensive. She has not joined any new organizations since becoming unemployed, but would like to join a gym as soon as it is viable. Going out to socialise required a trade-off situation "If I went out I had to miss out on something else due to the cost" (e.g. buy petrol or go to a pub with friends).

At present she reports that she is excited about beginning her traineeship and that she is very motivated, 'motivation is everything'. Deborah says she gets to the Job Club early in order to 'do a bit extra' towards starting her traineeship. She has begun re-establishing contact with several friends she has not seen for some time, but is still constrained by her financial situation.

Eileen, aged 19

Eileen was a secretary for a legal firm before being made redundant. She was initially angry and upset that she lost the position. She reported feeling 'shocked' and not expecting this to happen. Currently being unemployed does not 'really bother' Eileen. She has become less angry and now spends her time sending off letters and honing her interview technique.

She reports having had more interviews in the last six months than the previous six and feels her skills are improving. Due to an illness that occurred very soon after she lost her job Eileen did not actively pursue employment. It was almost nine months before she tried to obtain full time employment. Her job searching became serious at this point: she sent as many as thirty applications a week to prospective employers. Eileen set up a database on her computer to produce letters and keep track of applications. She does not cold canvas and only applies for vacancies. She has volunteered to do work in order to get experience and enhance her resumé.

Eileen encountered few frustrations when seeking employment. She reports that employers are unrealistic with expectations of experience for someone her age. No one her age could have the experience that they ask for. Whereas clothing for interviews was not an issue the cost of transport to so many interviews was.

Eileen copes with a reduced income by having an 'excessively organized budget'. She knows the best places to shop for budget food (she will not buy fruit from a supermarket, only from fruit/veggie shop). She has a travel allowance, a gift allowance and a drinks allowance. Eileen feels this budget is the only way to stretch the money. If Eileen and her boyfriend go out for lunch they will share a meal between the two of them. She is not interested in nightclubs or drinking at pubs. She will save a few weeks in advance for a dinner in town.

Leisure at home plays a large part in Eileen saving money. She will go around to friends' houses or they will come to hers. They offset the cost of videos/pizza by all contributing. She saw phone calls to friends were as a leisure activity. Eileen spends more time doing housework and practising her typing skills rather than watching television. She wants to keep busy rather that "watching Oprah all day". She watches less television and does more reading since becoming unemployed.

Not being employed created frustrations at home for Eileen. Both her father-in-law to be and mother-in-law to be "drove her up the wall" by hinting she was not trying hard enough to find a position. Her family were more supportive but there was tension between herself and her mother due to her moving out of the family home and in with her boyfriend before she had a full-time position.

Eileen's out-of-home activities were not affected too much. She reported not really going out "that much" before loosing her job, preferring to see friends at each other's homes. She has never played any sports. She says she "went somewhere nice" about four months previous to the interview, this was to a restaurant. Eileen says that on the whole her out-of-home leisure has not changed to any great degree since becoming unemployed, but special events tend to be slightly fewer and require more time to save for.

Eileen likes to keep herself busy. She believes she responds well to stress, but is also easy going so things don't bother her. She has become 'used to rejection' from prospective employers and now 'goes with the flow'. Eileen is confident that she will eventually obtain a position and this keeps her motivated and helps her not to become depressed about her situation. She believes that being realistic helps her cope.

The Job Club is providing Eileen with additional training in secretarial skills. The CES provides her with potential employers. She also says that her grandmother is supportive of her situation and she often talks to her about things. Her family in general is supportive. Eileen believes her friends are an external resource, her boyfriend in particular helps her cope. Her friends empathise with her situation and provide moral and social support.

Dawn, aged 20

Dawn reports that at first not having full time employment was 'all right', but now it is a 'pain'. She says that 'there is not as much money coming in and you get bored. Very bored'. Dawn would like a full time position not only to increase her income but also to meet some new people. She has been unemployed for over one year and she is sometimes depressed about her situation.

Dawn has tried several methods to obtain employment. The CES and Job Club are her main ways of trying to find a position. She has also completed two work courses at CES training centres. Dawn has sent out resumés, made phone calls, cold canvassed businesses and used the CES computer system. She finds that the computers are not very helpful.

Dawn's frustrations in obtaining employment include not having enough experience for prospective employers. She shares a car with other family members and this arrangement has not affected her ability to get to interviews. Initially she did not seek employment as keenly as she does now. At first she only applied for positions that interested her. As time progressed she began applying for any position she had a chance of obtaining, even if she did not fully fit the criteria. This was because she realised that she may not obtain a position she was 'interested' in as easily as she first thought.

Dawn coped with a reduced income by changing her entertainment and shopping habits. For example, if she was going out at night to pubs or nightclubs she would begin drinking at home before she went out because it was cheaper. When she was at the venue she would drink sparingly due to the prices of drinks. When shopping Dawn would 'only buy specials' and 'shop at certain supermarkets'. She reports not going out as much and not buying new clothes as much as she would like.

Her out-of-home activities have been affected to a small degree. She has played basketball for several years and has not had to give this up at this stage because of unemployment. Dawn reports having to 'cut back' on going out. Whereas she went out to venues on average three times a week, she now goes only once or twice and tries to spend as little as possible.

Dawn's family has on the whole been supportive. However, there have been periods of tension. Occasionally her parents will suggest she 'is not trying hard enough' to obtain a position. There are also difficulties if Dawn has to borrow money or cannot pay her bills. She reports no negative impact upon brothers and sisters, but concedes that on the whole it has been 'a negative thing'.

Leisure at home consists of some television (but no more that before becoming unemployed) and housework. Since both her parents are working full time, Dawn has taken on the role of completing the domestic chores. She will spend some time on the computer but says this is generally boring. Both the computer and videos are simply a way of "killing time". She admits to being 'really down' on occasions due to boredom. Dawn recently had to decline going overseas with some friends because of the cost. She sees friends less regularly now.

Dawn says that in general she cannot think of her "inner resources". When prompted she agrees that she is generally a positive person and knows she will eventually find a full time position. She agrees that she is motivated but does not elaborate, simply answering "yes" to the question.

Dawn enjoys going to the Skillshare. She appreciates this as an external resource and mentions that having stamps, envelopes and other stationery paid for is helpful. Friends also help by occasionally arranging for Dawn to do a day or two's work at their places of employment in order to earn extra money and gain experience. She appreciates her family sometimes lending her money when she needs it.

Loren, aged 18

Loren's job loss was voluntary. She moved from interstate during this period to Western Australia and reports being upset at having to leave because she enjoyed the work and missed the people she worked with. Loren was very anxious about the future and was "uncomfortable" about not having work when she arrived. She has been unemployed for over six months and "I am at the point that now where I can't do anything more to look for a job. I've gone everywhere and done everything I can think of". Loren misses being occupied. She says that on occasion she feels depressed.

Loren began searching for work by registering with the CES. They did not help much. She has compiled resumés and walked into businesses and handed them to prospective employers. She has also looked through the Yellow Pages and the job section of the West Australian newspaper. Loren is frustrated and angry about what she perceives to be employer bias: "... some employers go for looks. They don't really look at the quality and what someone can do". Loren has to borrow clothes from friends for interviews. She reports seeking work even more keenly than three months ago. She is completing a child-care course in order to enhance her prospects.

Loren is not sure how she makes her income stretch. She says she is "just not spending". "Most people go to the movies every day or buy cigarettes or magazines, I just don't do any of that. I don't waste my money on stuff I don't need". Loren shops at the cheaper supermarkets. She does not "go out much". Her reduced income has meant entertainment has been cut to a minimum, less pubs and nightclubs. She can no longer "go out whenever I like".

Her family saw Loren's unemployment as "a big bonus because I'm doing the housework". Loren reports her family as being generally supportive. She does not have transport and members of her family will drive her to job interviews. They will also lend her money if she has to take public transport or a taxi. There is no tension about Loren's position.

On top of the housework, unemployment has also impacted upon other aspects of Loren's home activities. She does not watch television during the day. She sees herself as a very "interactive person" and thus uses the phone to talk to friends when unable to visit them. She cannot usually afford to join them on nights out in town. If she "hasn't got anything to do I sit and read a book".

Outside the home Loren has had to give up her sporting commitments (netball) because of the cost associated with playing. Rather than sit at home, she will walk around the city or a park. Less money has meant not going out to socialise as much as she would like. She can no longer 'go out when I want'. Transport is also an issue since Loren does not own a car.

From an inner strengths perspective Loren was very forthcoming about her feelings. She is positive; 'I'm going to keep going until I get a job. I don't put myself down. I just think positive the whole time'. She does not want to be perceived as a 'dole bludger'. She wants people to understand she is really looking hard, but it is difficult. Loren is enthusiastic about applying for positions and confidant about her eventual success. She confesses to being angry at the media for portraying unemployed people in a negative light. She feels they should be more supportive. Searching is "getting her down" but she says she is resilient.

Her external resources include family who provide transport and money as well as friends who provide 'emotional support' and sometimes attend interviews with her. Both the Skillshare and CES have provided Loren with training and avenues for potential positions.

Sandra, aged 19

Sandra has only had part-time employment. She has been searching for a full time position and has had several interviews. Sandra reports not having full-time employment as 'not good', money is a difficulty as most of it goes towards bills. She says that even having a 'spare $5' is unusual. She is not angry about unemployment as she knows it is not her fault.

Sandra finds job searching is frustrating for a number of reasons. Lack of experience is "really disappointing" as she feels it is not possible to have the amount employers seem to want. Sandra reports that three months previously she was disappointed at not having found a position but is hopeful about the next three. Steps she has taken include knocking on doors and checking local shopping centre notice boards. Local newspapers, CES, help from father and sending out resumés all form part of her job searching. Transport is an issue. Sandra says that using public transport is unreliable and she is sometimes late for an interview. It may take her as much as three hours to get to an interview using public transport. Sandra still seeks work as keenly as she did three months previously.

Sandra copes with a reduced income by "not spending and only paying people I owe". She also no longer goes out on weekdays because "... you just walk down the street, you need money". Sandra's mother will buy her clothes if she requires them for interviews. Friends will often pay for Sandra to go out. She reports going out only 'every couple of weeks'.

Sandra's mother and father are also employed part-time. They are supportive and help by looking out for potential positions for Sandra. She currently lives at home and believes that no friction arises because of her unemployment.

Leisure at home consists of "ringing lots of people" and watching more television. She will watch television until late at night and will read 'all the time'. Sandra will also listen to the radio. She reports doing more general housework and will "clean the house to help out a bit".

Sandra's out-of-home leisure has been heavily affected because of the lack of money. She has 'stopped going to the movies' and walks around more. Her sporting commitments have suffered due more to lack of time than money. Commitment to TAFE and Skillshare means she has no time for out-of-home activities at present, but she says it is worth it in order to build up a resumé. Lack of time has affected her relationships with friends, as they become angry and feel that Sandra does not want to go out with them. This frustrates her.

When asked about personal traits she replied "enthusiasm" and "motivation". She believes that potential employers pick up on motivated people so she tries to convey this. A "positive outlook" is a strength. "If you get setbacks you just have to say hey, don't worry, just get back up". "You focus on the next job". She does not want to be perceived as a "dole bludger". She thinks people should "walk a mile in my shoes".

Sandra reports a range of skills she hopes will help her find employment including "baby-sitting and typing skills". Friends and family are an important external resource. They provide emotional support as well as financial. Friends will give Sandra lifts to interviews. Sandra thinks Social Security and Skillshare are useful support services. Job Link is also an avenue Sandra has utilised. Friends may tell Sandra about potential positions.

Vanessa, aged 24

Vanessa was upset at losing her job. She felt "all over the place" and was not able to get over the short notice she was given. She reports "having to walk out". Other words Vanessa uses to describe the experience include "angry", "anxious" and "stressed". She had these feelings "all at once". It was a particularly difficult time psychologically.

Vanessa's job search was "very stressful". She reports a "constant, every day stress" having to go through the job search process. She said she felt worse three months ago. Completing a course with Skillshare has improved her outlook. Vanessa has 'something to look forward to'. Three months before "I didn't have any prospects or encouragement. I didn't know what I wanted to do either and jobs are very hard to find". There has been a gradual improvement as she goes through the process of interviews. Vanessa still does not feeling confident that she will succeed, she believes she needs more skills in order to be successful. Her job search included looking in the newspaper, contacting the CES, and phone calls. She no longer sends out resumés; "I don't send out resumés any more because you don't get a reply". Vanessa has never obtained an interview out by sending a cold canvass resumé. She has been given interviews by turning up in person and inquiring if a position is available.

Reduced income simply means "cutting back on everything". Vanessa no longer "goes shopping (presumably for non-essential items)" or goes to the movies. She will buy Black and Gold brand food and cheaper items. Vanessa will make lunch rather than buy it because of expense. Petrol is an expense so she "drives around" less. Time outside of the house is planned in order to cut down on petrol usage. Vanessa does not "go out for drinks as much". Later she said she no longer goes out at all. With no sporting interests she has not had to cut back in this area.

She has had some difficulties at home. She says that her mother "wasn't too stressed because she trusts me be able to help out". As long as she can pay her share of the bills she feels her mother will be supportive. Her mother is 'snappy' on occasions. Vanessa reports being more tired and anxious in general. She seems to "catch everything that is going around".

At home Vanessa does more housework in order to contribute to the running of the family home. She says "I've got into reading" since having more time at home. Vanessa watches the same amount of television as she did before becoming unemployed. In order to 'kill time' Vanessa will spend more time with her pets. Her activities outside the home have also been affected. She does not go out as much due to entertainment costs. She is "bored because I don't get to meet anyone". Leisure consists of cheaper activities such as walking her dogs on the beach, both for the exercise and to simply "get out of the house". Vanessa can still afford to go to the movies "once in a blue moon". She is now "used to being poor" and not going to those venues she used to before she lost her job.

Vanessa identified patience as an inner resource, "I'm patient. I will wait for a job". She also reports being motivated, but admits to getting "down occasionally, but I put on a good act for people ...". Her external resources include a group called Work Right. This organization "does everything" including helping you with your social life. She says her mother 'helps a lot' as well as the CES. Vanessa regrets that her friends are not an external resource. When she lost her position they "didn't want to see me". They were going out and did not have time for her. Vanessa is disappointed that unemployment had this impact upon her friends and social life. This has affected her motivation. There are days she cannot leave the house because of the lack of motivation to seek work. Vanessa misses the routine a job provided as well as the security to "plan ahead for things" that a steady income provides.

Melanie, aged 18

Melanie voluntarily left her last position because of the lack of potential for advancement. She enrolled in TAFE in order to enhance her job prospects. Melanie is currently completing a course at the Job Club. She says "I really don't like not having a job". Melanie wants full time work, not only for the financial security it would provide but also for the structure a full time position gives: "...it would give me something to do during the day so I wouldn't be so bored". Money and structure would allow Melanie to be "my own person and get my routine happening'. She would often sleep late with the feeling of "what's the point of trying?."

Three months before Melanie reports said she was "really agitated" about not having full-time employment. She was angry and "grumpy all the time". Melanie was being interviewed "heaps" but had not been successful. This was becoming stressful and she reports becoming depressed at her lack of success. She felt in a rut, particularly since her friends who were also unemployed were obtaining positions. Melanie is less stressed and anxious being at the Job Club at present and doing occasional relief work.

Her search has included "word of mouth", just asking people if work is available. She said she would be happy doing "anything". Melanie looks in newspapers and listens to the radio (a Perth radio station was running a job telethon at the time of the interview). She has made her own "calling cards", which she distributes to businesses. Melanie has also sent out resumés on a cold canvass basis as well as put notices on local notice boards. Some major frustrations in job searching include "the rejection, that's the main thing". Rejection affected her confidence. She would often ring employers when she had not been successful in order to get some feedback as to why she had. Having to use public transport was a difficulty, both the time it took to get to interviews and the cost. Melanie reports seeking work more keenly than she did three months ago because she felt more confident.

Melanie's reduced income meant she had to "put (herself) on a budget". Bills and rent were a priority, any remaining money would be divided into entertainment or saving for a specific item. She could not go shopping for luxuries such as new clothes. She would occasionally go to the movies if her boyfriend would pay. Melanie's mother did all the food shopping from the rent money. She has not being able to save for a holiday or go "clubbing" with her friends. Melanie has no sporting commitments, however she would like to try horseriding if she could afford to start.

Her family put "a lot of pressure" on her to get a full time position. It was upsetting and caused Melanie to move away from home for a short period. Her mother was particularly upset that she had voluntarily left her last position without having another one to go to. Her lack of money caused her to return to the family home. This was a particularly negative time for the family.

Melanie's activities at home increased – she did "heaps of stuff at home" – much more domestic work. More television initially but then "I got sick of it so I stopped watching altogether". She replaced this by listening to the radio and reading quite extensively. Her out-of-home activities were affected to the extent that she would still go out but did not spend money at the venues. She and her friends would also go to cheaper venues such as the beach or nightclubs that had free entry. They would also stay at 'each others places' in order to decrease the cost of socialising.

Melanie identifies herself as having 'heaps of confidence' at present. She tries to be positive but occasionally gets 'down.' Her external resources include friends who 'build me back up if I lose confidence and give up hope'. She reports relying on them heavily to 'be there for her' if she has not been successful in obtaining a position. They help keep her motivated and her self-esteem up. Her family tends to play the same role. The Job Club and CES have been helpful.

Tracy, aged 23

Tracy feels "bad" about not having full-time employment. Her position started as full-time but has been reduced in hours which was making it difficult to live. Tracy simply feels "really down" about her situation. It is affecting her self-esteem and confidence. She reports not understanding why she has not been successful to date. Tracy is unsure whether it is because she is 'not good enough' or whether her lack of experience is playing against her. Three months before the interview Tracy said she did not feel as 'bad' as she does at present. Her condition has changed due to the number of "negative responses" she has been receiving from prospective employers. The consistent rejection has affected her motivation to continue trying as hard as she had previously. Tracy uses words such as "depressed" and "angry" to describe how she feels.

Her job search has consisted of sending out letters (Tracy estimates over 100 to date), cold canvassing businesses, telephone calls and looking through the jobs section of the newspaper. She has also "knocked on doors" and left her resumé at businesses. She finds personal presentation the hardest for fear of being "embarrassed". The two main frustrations she has encountered have been lack of qualifications and "not enough skills". Tracy wants to leave the sales area but does not have a skills base in any other area and is encountering difficulty. She identifies experience as the "number one thing" that prospective employers require. Whereas money for transport or petrol was not a problem for her, not being able to buy clothes for interviews was. Tracy does voluntary work in order to gain experience.

Reduced income is a difficulty for Tracy. She has to on occasion to "beg parents for money". She reports having a personal loan and making repayments is "very, very difficult". If her parents were not supportive, Tracy considers she would not "get through". Tracy will shop at cheaper supermarkets as well as buy cheaper clothes when she needs to. Reduced income means less entertainment: Tracy will "just stay home sometimes you just can't afford it, which is very, very bad". She does not go out as much as she would like. Tracy believes she is not "entitled" to those things she was used to when she was employed. Her words were, "you're not entitled to loans at all or credit cards, or anything like that". Tracy has had to give up the gym due to not being able to afford the membership. Other effects of unemployment include not being able to live by herself, not being able to "look after yourself", and not being able to "dress better".

Tracy wishes to be independent but not having a full-time position has made this impracticable. She cannot leave home and has to "live under their rules". Being dependent on her family makes her feel "like a child" and "... you can't feel good about yourself...". Full time employment would mean independence for Tracy. In general she thinks her family are not very supportive. They "keep on pushing me everyday". They "think I don't try enough (to get employment)". She feels this is unfair and is causing arguments and stress within the family. Tracy believes that her parents do not appreciate her situation. Her relationship with her boyfriend is also strained because of the lack of money. She does not want him to "look after her", but cannot be independent at present. They use the one income for entertainment.

Tracy reports being at home more and will often "just clean the house" for something to do. She will watch television, read, and listen to the radio. Tracy does not like being without the structure a full-position would provide. She would also like to get married next year but not having a full-time position will probably prevent.

Tracey's out-of-home activities have suffered. She cannot "go out to lunch with friends". She cannot go to the gym. Her friends offer to "treat" her to lunch but she declines "feeling bad" about not being able to pay for herself. She says, "I'm withdrawing myself, you know".

When asked about personal traits Tracy replied that "I don't have any strengths really...I'm really down about it (unemployment)". When prompted Tracy concedes that she is motivated. She identifies patience as a personal trait. She also reports she is basically positive about the future and has not completely given up. Her external resources include friends and the Job Club. Her friends are supportive and "make me feel better". They help Tracy prepare resumés and applications on their computers. She speaks of her family as "kind of supportive".

The essence of each of these experiences of unemployment is summarised and presented in Table 6.1, so that similarities and differences in impact can be seen.

Table 6.1
Impacts of Unemployment for Selected Variables for Females

	Unemployment impact	Job search	Reduced income	Family relationships / responsibilities	Activities at home	Out-of-home activities	Personal resources	External resources
Lesley 19 years	Loss of security; relief with pregnancy; depressed & suicidal; over time more positive, enthusiastic.	Skills acquired at job club; intensive search for jobs, phone, letter, fax; lack of transport, interview clothing, qualifications, experience.	Bought second-hand clothes; cheaper supermarkets; less going out; less toys for daughter; bill-paying by instalments.	Lack of transport to visit parents; boyfriend supportive; envy of sisters' & brother's employment.	Looking after daughter; electronic games; gardening; reduced drinking & entertainment.	Cheaper forms of recreation – visiting parks & jetty.	Independent; kept busy; enjoy 'everyday stuff'; positive, enthusiastic.	Family & friends; employment & job training agencies.
Marion 23 years	Demoralised, depressed; lacked motivation, energy, wanted to stay in bed longer.	Actively sought work, but with several rejections stopped trying; lacked qualifications and experience.	Everyday living difficult; hard to pay transport, rent, general bills; demoralised by lack of money; tight budget.	Parents anxious; seen by them not to be trying to get a job; family threats causes physical withdrawal.	More TV, video, phone & computer activities causing increased bills; frowned by parents; did house cleaning but no recognition from parents.	Lack of money caused curtailment of sporting activities; felt uncomfortable with friends.	Sense of hope with persistence & better outlook in life – but self-esteem down & depression continues.	Family & friends generally supportive.

	Unemployment impact	Job search	Reduced income	Family relationships / responsibilities	Activities at home	Out-of-home activities	Personal resources	External resources
Deborah 21 years	Deprivation of income, socialising structure & routine of job resulting in being 'down'.	Restaurant trainee through job club; unanswered letters, phone calls led to frustration; lack of interview clothing & cost of petrol affected job search.	Survival on necessities – food, electricity & petrol; lifestyle changed to cheap foods, less socialising & entertainment.	Borrowing money from father caused friction; being home & sullen added to difficulties with him.	More TV, computer games, videos; drinking intensified alongside depression.	Unable to play netball because of transportation, equipment and ancillary costs; less nightclubs, pubs, but went to cheap parties.	Recently motivated to participate in the work force; positive & has priorities.	Job club; father; beginning to re-establish contact with friends after drinking & depression problems.
Eileen 21 years	Initially angry & upset, but long-term illness followed. Over time 'used to rejection'.	Acquired skills at job club; sent resumé, made phone calls, looked through the paper; did volunteer work; did not cold canvas.	Devised a budget; shopped at cheaper outlets; stayed home more; pooled money with friends for entertainment at home.	Boyfriend, grandmother supportive, but parents in law less supportive; friction with mother over lifestyle.	Domestic chores increased; less TV but more reading; more time on phone & computer; met friends at home rather than outside home.	Not involved in sports or clubs; but went out less but had to save to do so.	Motivated; not easily depressed; positive about the future.	Job club and employment agency. Particularly supportive - boyfriend and grandmother.
Dawn 20 years	Initially not concerned; now more	Gained skills at job club; phone calls, letters,	Generally at home; no new clothes; cheaper	Relationship with parents strained; seen	More domestic chores; more TV & computer	Still plays sport, but goes out less; missed	Motivated & positive; confident	Money from family; work experience

	Unemployment impact	Job search	Reduced income	Family relationships / responsibilities	Activities at home	Out-of-home activities	Personal resources	External resources
	worried seeking work more keenly; occasionally depressed & 'down', but still positive.	resumés, & work experience; applying for positions despite not fulfilling criteria.	supermarkets & less spending when out.	not to be trying hard enough; adopted role of housekeeper.	games; will drink at home rather than out to save money.	holiday in Bali because of lack of money.	about future employment.	with friends; uses job club, employment agency and labour market training facilities.
Loren 18 years	Upset, anxious & misses social contact at work; Still positive about the future.	On a training course; uses job club & training facilities to seek work; visits potential employers, uses the phone & newspaper.	Buys cheaper food; less socialising with friends; going out curtailed.	Supportive family with money & transport; friend supportive too.	More domestic tasks; increase in reading, phone calls but not TV.	Sporting commitment given up because of cost; cheaper forms of recreation such as walking; less socialising with friends.	Strong-willed, motivated and positive about the future; resents 'dole bludger' tag.	Employment agency not helpful, but job training facility, family and friends are supportive.
Sandra 19 years	Disappointed, but job loss not her fault; motivated, expects to be employed.	Frustrating; transport difficulties; disappointed with level of experience expected by employers;	Bill-paying a priority; little left for entertainment; dependent on mother for clothes.	Family supportive emotionally & financially; friends supportive, but lack of money	Keeps in social contact over the phone; More TV, reading and house to help out; listens to radio sometimes.	Activities curtailed as time spent increasing job skills; less time for sport & friends; lack	Motivated with a positive attitude; seeks work keenly despite period without work; setbacks get her down, but still	Family, friends, TAFE, job marketing training office, employment agency, and

	Unemployment impact	Job search	Reduced income	Family relationships / responsibilities	Activities at home	Out-of-home activities	Personal resources	External resources
		technical & job market training will help.		causes friction at times.		of money means weekdays home.	positive.	job club. Friends helpful for job opportunities.
Vanessa 24 years	Psychologically badly affected; angry, anxious, over stressed; over time regaining motivation, but has 'down' days.	Improving skills for resumé; work experience stressful; still lacks confidence.	Shops at cheaper markets; Cut back on entertainment, going out with friends; lunch at home to save costs; petrol rationed.	More housework; family supportive; tired around the home; friends not so supportive.	More reading, housework, time with pets; TV generally the same.	Going to cheaper venues; walking the dog; occasional movies, but generally homebound.	Motivation & confidence has ups and downs. Hopes to be ultimately successful.	Employment agency and job training office; Family a resource, but not friends.
Melanie 18 years	Employment agency and job training office; Family a resource, but not friends.	Employment agency and job training office; Family a resource, but not friends.	Back to family home; budgets – bills, rent are priorities; cheaper venues; holiday deferred.	Cause of family stress; negative impact; pressure by mother to find work.	More domestic work; more reading, radio, but less TV; friends come to home rather than seek entertainment outside home.	Go out less, but to cheaper venues; no sporting commitments; horseriding lessons postponed.	Presently confident & positive; occasionally 'gets down'; postive about the future.	Relies heavily on family, friends to keep her motivated; Uses employment agency & job club.

	Unemployment impact	Job search	Reduced income	Family relationships / responsibilities	Activities at home	Out-of-home activities	Personal resources	External resources
Tracy 23 years	Angry & depressed; self-esteem, confidence affected; constant rejection affects motivation adversely.	Lack of experience a serious problem; sends resumés, cold canvasses, phones businesses, looks through newspaper.	Dependent on parents for money; cheaper supermarkets, clothes; ineligible for credit cards & loans.	Family arguments, stress; boyfriend supportive, but relationship affected by less money; setback to wedding plans.	More domestic work, TV, reading & listening to radio.	Lunch with friends, gym attendance curtailed; unable to accept & reciprocate friends' hospitality.	Patient, motivated and positive about the future; keen to be independent.	Friends emotionally supportive, biggest resource; family also a resource but not totally supportive.

Males

Doug, aged 20

Doug reported being angry and sad at loosing his last position. It was a particularly difficult time, given that he had moved from his family to a country region in order to start this new job. He thought that "everything was going well" just before his retrenchment. Losing his job had an immediate financial impact on Doug and affected him psychologically because the family depended on him to be the breadwinner.

Doug is not fluent in English. He compiled his own resumé, but felt it was not appropriate. He is presently in a Job Club where he has been assisted in compiling a suitable resumé. This resumé has been sent out to various prospective employers. He cold canvasses and applies for vacancies from the newspaper. He is not confident phoning potential employers because of his lack of fluency in English.

He has encountered very few frustrations to date in his job search. He "always has money for petrol". He owns his car and has a number of suitable clothes for interviews. Doug has always searched for employment 'very keenly'. He has currently stopped searching until he has finished a two-week computer course at the Job Club.

Doug's reduced income has also had an impact upon his life-style. He reports having to "watch money". He does not drive his car as much to entertainment venues because of the cost of fuel. Luxury items and expensive foods cannot be bought on his budget. Doug will only buy "necessities". Both Doug and his wife save enough money to take their young son out once a week. They may go to cheaper or free venues, such as simply going into the city.

Lack of full time work has had a negative impact upon Doug's family. He reports his wife and son looking 'sad, you know, because we don't do things we normally could'.

Table 6.2

Impact of Unemployment on Selected Variables for Males

	Unemployment impact	*Job search*	*Reduced income*	*Family relationships / responsibilities*	*Activities at home*	*Out-of-home activities*	*Personal resources*	*External resources*
Doug 20 years	Immediate financial impact; Angry & sad at job loss; undue pressure to provide for family.	Relies on job training; difficulties with the English language causes problems approaching employers.	Buys necessities; can't afford expensive foods or luxuries, or to take family out; depends on free venues.	Sadness noticed with wife & children, but no real family tensions.	More gardening & general small jobs around the house; does not watch TV or reads books.	Cheaper forms of recreation; visits to parks, city, cycling & jogging; not a member of clubs or associations.	Motivated; tends to read books with positive messages.	Relies at job training place for skills; appreciates social contact there.
Bret 18 years	Loss of financial security &future direction; disappointment with travel plans; seeks works keenly, but now becoming desperate.	A variety of methods used – job training, employment agency, word-of-mouth, cold canvassing; disappointment with requirement of increased skill levels.	'Going out 'curtailed; tight budget, depends on family for transport & financial assistance; gym membership lapsed.	Family supportive, but occasional friction & stress; negative impact on the whole.	Home more often; more home jobs, gardening, odd jobs, but less TV; prefers 'things with hands' – fixing car, art work.	Cheaper forms – bike-riding, walking; sees friends less, not able to afford costs at go-karting, pot black venues.	Motivated & positive; feels he will eventually obtain a job; occasionally 'down', but has a 'never give up' attitude.	Employment & training agency; family & girlfriend for emotional support.

	Unemployment impact	Job search	Reduced income	Family relationships / responsibilities	Activities at home	Out-of-home activities	Personal resources	External resources
Carl 18 years	Disappointed, anxious & angry; seeks work keenly.	Word of mouth & work site visits; contact with past employers; goes for advertised positions; delayed replies & rejections causes frustrating, disappointing.	Unable to afford interview clothes, repair car & purchase preferred drinks; socialises with friends & takes girlfriend out less often.	Financial difficulties with single-parent mother, but she is generally supportive; social discomfort causes fewer visits to relatives.	More housework, TV listening to stereo; gave up guitar lessons; homebound & consequently enjoys weekends less.	Goes out less; visits friends at home rather than elsewhere; cheaper forms of recreation, beach, park etc.	Generally positive, but gets 'down'; motivated & keen, feels 'like shit' due to constant job search.	Family, friends, girlfriend for emotional & practical support; employment & job training agencies major resources.
Bruno 18 years	Angry, worried & confused; anxious about financial future; desperate to get work, but positive about achieving a full time job.	Started immediately at job club; frustration include inability to afford petrol to get to interviews; disappointment being turned down.	Spends & socialises less; depends on parents of financial support.	Family supportive, occasional friction, but limited to 'nagging'.	More domestic chores, TV, videos & listening to music; strives to be out of home to avoid being in a rut.	Driving around, but less because can't afford fuel; sees friends less, but sporting commitments still pursued as before.	Motivated, relates to people, but shy; positive but anxious to gain employment; self-esteem affected but does not deter job search.	Social security & job training; family & friends provide emotional & practical support.

	Unemployment impact	Job search	Reduced income	Family relationships / responsibilities	Activities at home	Out-of-home activities	Personal resources	External resources
Walter 25 years	Initial stress & anxiety about financial position; felt rejected & self-confidence affected.	Relies on friends' help; Uses employment agency, job training & recently cold canvassing.	Buys less for himself; cannot afford socialising with friends, buying petrol & clothes for interviews.	Lives alone, but father supportive.	More TV, videos; sleeps more to 'kill a few hours'. Occasionally gardens; misses daily work structure.	Job loss has minimal impact; fishes, swims, walks & dives as before job loss.	Tolerant & patient; confident of success in landing a job; self-esteem & confidence would be higher then.	Employment agency, job club & friends for financial support & casual work; Father helpful too.
Simon 29 years	Angry & in financial difficulty; was depressed which motivated job search; since found some motivation.	Used employment agency, phone calls, letters, visiting businesses, & Internet; frustrations intensified by the use of public transport & not owning a car.	Car repossessed; has moved back to family home; no luxury goods, less entertainment & no social life.	Some 'nagging' from family, but generally supportive; lost contact with friends.	More computer activity for entertain-ment, preparing resumés & letters; Less TV, more reading, listening to radio; some odd jobs at home.	Cheaper activities, walking on beach with walkman; less pubs, nightclubs, but had no prior sporting commitments during employment.	Motivate & persistent; has acquired more 'people skills'.	Family, employment agency & job club.

	Unemployment impact	Job search	Reduced income	Family relationships / responsibilities	Activities at home	Out-of-home activities	Personal resources	External resources
Rodger 24 years	Initially 'confused'; stressed & anxious about future; job club involvement has reduced anxiety.	Completed reskilling course; Uses employment agency; job club, newspapers & sends resumés; frustrated with time spent for little reward.	Less entertainment; looks for food bargains; luxury items such as CDs unaffordable; more time given for voluntary activity – scouts.	Helps around the house with domestic chores; living at home; family financially & emotionally understanding & supportive	TV & reading the same as before unemployment.	Goes out less; goes to venues close to home; given up canoeing because of cost of equipment & transport; entertainment restricted.	Patient, but motivated; confident to obtain a job eventually.	Involvement with scouts to 'take mind off things'; family, friends, employment agency; job club.
Justin 20 years	Initially unconcerned, but over time become anxious about the future; motivation adversely affected, but is gaining confidence.	Job club, employment agency & newspapers; lack of experience & qualifications are problems; changing appearance for interviews worrying.	Back to family home; uses concession card for public transport; less entertainment in & out of home; eats lower quality food, buys necessities.	Causing his family stress, but they are generally supportive, although don't understand what he wants.	Photography & painting ceased; more gardening; listening to music; TV same as before unemployment.	Pubs & dinners stopped, but walking on the beach continued.	Considers himself 'emotionally balanced', not easily down; positive & meditates to cope.	Job club, employment agency; family for emotional & practical support; friends for casual work & information.

	Unemployment impact	*Job search*	*Reduced income*	*Family relationships / responsibilities*	*Activities at home*	*Out-of-home activities*	*Personal resources*	*External resources*
Gordon 22 years	Extreme disappointment & frustration; personal goals affected, unable to plan; misses social contact at work.	Employment agency & job club; relies on cold canvassing; non-responses from employers annoying & frustrating.	Budget prioritised; payment of board to family postponed; looks for lower price shopping.	Frustrations taken out on the family, but they are supportive.	Creates & produces music; uses computer, reads more, but watches less TV.	Sporting commitments still maintained – basketball in the park; goes out less with mates; visits friends because it is cheap.	Positive outlook, does not get depressed; basically happy and confident.	Family & some friends supportive; employment and training agencies important practical resources.
Wayne 21 years	Not concerned at first, but over time anxious & pessimistic; angry at not having full time work; misses time structure of employment.	Employment agency; job club, cold canvassing, Internet & word of mouth; "doing as much as he can...".	Buys less, unable to save for car, spends less on weekends, girlfriend, but still continues sporting commitment.	Family supportive, but unsure what his parents think.	Reads more, but did not identify other activities.	Goes out less & activities adversely affected by unemployment.	Positive & determined; self-perceived perseverance as an important trait; tends not to be 'down' or depressed.	Family & girlfriend provide emotional support; friends give practical support; job club, employment agency & leisure activities.

Doug's activities in the home increased after he lost his full time work. He did more gardening and general housework. Although he does read and watch television his main leisure activity is gardening. His activities outside the home were also affected. Entertainment consisted of cheaper or free venues. Doug and his family will go to the beach or a park. For fitness Doug will go cycling or for walks.

Doug believes he is generally a positive person. He reads "books with a positive attitude" (it is not clear if he means self-help books). His wife looks after the budget. Doug's external resources include Skillshare, which he says he attends every day in order to improve his computer skills and compile his resumé as well as send letters to prospective employers. He feels that being with 'positive people' in the same situation as he is in helps him stay focused about continuing to try to obtain a position. Since his family is in Czechoslovakia and he has few friends in Australia he likes the social aspect of Skillshare.

Bret, aged 18

Bret voluntarily gave up his last position because he was "not getting along with anyone". He suffered a degree of stress not having an income and not "knowing where (he was) going ...because the main part of your life is your job". The particular circumstances that led Bret to quit made him "very annoyed", but he was confident that "something was going to come along sooner or later". Bret said he felt very anxious being down to the "bare limits" in his bank account and accumulating debts.

Bret's job search has included using the facilities of the CES. He knows people in the industry he wishes to gain full-time employment in and has asked them to "keep an eye open" for him. He has sent out his resumé to businesses and writes cold canvass letters, as well as using the newspaper. Bret has been frustrated by the requirement of experience by potential employers. He feels he will not be successful unless he completes a course in order to show he has some experience in the field. Bret seeks work more keenly now than three months before. He is "desperate" about obtaining a position.

A reduced income has impacted upon Bret's lifestyle. He reports not going out on weekends due to lack of money – "you have to stick on a really tight budget". Bret receives a great deal of help from his parents. They will give him lifts to interviews and occasionally offer financial support. Bret has had to give up going to the gym due to the cost of membership. He has also had to give up socialising as much with friends because the venues they choose to go to. He cannot afford to go to Pot-Black, McDonald's or Go-Karting.

His family has not been overly affected by Bret's unemployment. He says his parents are "pretty casual" about his situation, but there have been periods when he has been depressed about unemployment and this has "brought the family down and then tempers just start...". He reports a negative impact on the whole family, but they are still more supportive than not.

Bret is at home much more due to unemployment. He says he "helps a lot more around the house", working in the garden, and doing general odd jobs. Bret does not watch television or listen to the radio very much. He prefers activities at home that utilise his skills with his hands. He "works on his car" and "scribbles a lot on pads". Out of home activities tend to include "just riding my bike around the area" or walking. Bret cannot go out to pubs and nightclubs with friends due to the cost. At present the only sporting commitment he has had to give up is his gym membership, however, he is not sure whether his financial position will affect his playing football when the season starts.

Bret identifies fulfilling his goals as a difficulty associated with unemployment. He cannot save for a new car, or afford to fix up the one he has. He can also no longer plan to travel.

Unemployment has "slowed me down in a lot of ways, not being able to plan for the future is a frustration and disappointment".

Bret's inner resources tend to include a positive attitude. He believes that you should "never give up no matter how down you get or whatever just never...". Bret is persistent and tries to stay motivated. If he feels down he makes a point of building himself back up. His external resources include the CES, newspapers and word-of-mouth, as well as phone calls and sending of resumés. He identifies the Job Club as a resource. Bret considers his girlfriend and family as a support simply because they "are just there" they help to take his mind of his situation.

Carl, aged 18

When Carl was retrenched, he was 'pretty sad" that this had happened because he was "really liking the job". Carl was disappointed that he had to begin to search for another full-time position. He was often angry at himself because he could not secure a full-time job and does not like the questions and feedback he receives from family and friends. They would ask if he was looking hard enough or ask why he had not found work. Carl found this frustrating. He also reports becoming stressed and anxious about his situation.

Carl's job search has included visiting 'job sites' and speaking to people in the industry. This word-of-mouth approach has worked on previous occasions. He has also contacted previous employers to let them know he is available. Whereas he has not sent out cold canvass resumés and letters, Carl has sent applications for advertised positions in the paper. The CES and Job Club have also been avenues he has utilised. Some frustrations associated with his job search have included the constant disappointment of not being successful for a position, especially when "you think you have a really good chance". Carl identifies waiting as a particular frustration.

Practical frustrations include lack of money for petrol and public transport. He feels he may do better in interviews if he could afford the style of clothing he would like to wear.

Carl says he is seeking work just as keenly now as he did when he first lost his position. A reduced income has impacted on various aspects of Carl's life. He copes by "spending as little as possible", particularly on fuel and entertainment (although he identifies 'going out' as important). Carl's parents "help out", he will also buy the "cheapest clothes and alcohol". Lack of money has meant he cannot repair his car which further affects his ability to get to job interviews. Lack of income has basically meant that Carl "can't buy what I want to buy. I can't buy the clothes I want. I can't buy the alcohol I want. I can't buy things for my car". He cannot afford to take his girlfriend nightclubbing.

Unemployment has impacted upon his family – "It sort of made us struggle a bit because I've got a single parent". It is difficult for them to pay the bills as well as afford to help Carl financially. He reports his mother as "really trying" and she is supportive of his situation. There are occasional arguments about "not trying hard enough (to find a job)". Carl does not visit other members of his family not feeling "confident" with no full-time work. He says he would visit them more often if he was employed as this would mean he would not have to answer "those questions. About what to do you do...".

Carl helps around the house more often now that he is at home more. He will "clean the house" just to do something. He reports "definitely watching more television than when I was working". He will also listen to his stereo, but does not read books. Carl is "not into gardening". He was learning the guitar but has had to stop, because he cannot afford lessons.

Activities outside of his home were affected. Carl says "I can't go out and have as much fun as I want". He enjoys his weekends less. He will go to friends' houses for drinks, but if they decide to go to an expensive venue he will not go with them. He also reports he cannot have as good a time with his girlfriend as he could when employed. Carl does not "have as much money as I want and need" to go out with friends and girlfriend.

Carl identifies his girlfriend as a resource "because she knows I'm looking and that helps". He feels he should not be angry with himself for not obtaining a position due to the fact he is trying and has a positive feeling about the amount of effort he is putting into the search – "I'm fairly motivated but every now and again you just think I haven't got a job... and you just feel like shit". Carl has been "depressed" every now and again but lifts himself out of it. External resources include friends (who give lifts for job interviews), the Job Club, CES and his mother.

Bruno, aged 18

Bruno reported being "confused" when he was informed that he had lost his position. He was worried about the future and what lay ahead. Bruno was particularly angry because he felt he lost his job unfairly. He had immediate thoughts of financial difficulties and about "running out of money" before he was successful in obtaining another full-time position. Bruno was less worried and anxious three months previous to the interview. He was concerned and said: "I'm pretty much desperate now to get a job".

Bruno's job search meant that he went "straight into action" as soon as he no longer had work. He immediately registered with Social Security and was referred to the Job Club. At present the Job Club is the only step Bruno has taken to find work. He has not made phone calls, preferring to "see where (the Job Club) is going to lead me". Frustrations with search include not being able to afford petrol for his car and public transport being "a bit of a problem", both in terms of cost and convenience. Bruno identifies "being turned down' as a frustration. He often becomes "down" when this occurs.

Bruno has secured a part-time position, but the income from this job is barely enough. Coping with a reduced income means simply "spending less". He reports liking to "drive a lot" (for leisure) but can no longer do this due to the cost of fuel. Bruno "socialises less" due to the cost of going out. His parents pick up the cost of food and board, Bruno can only afford to pay $50 a week. He had no sporting commitments prior to losing his job and has not had to give any up.

It would appear that Bruno's circumstances have not affected the family to a great degree. He believes they are "very supportive", they have on occasions been "naggy" but this is due to them "really want(ing) me to get a job". Bruno considers they appreciate how hard it is to find a position and respect the fact he is "trying his best" to find one.

Bruno's activities at home include more domestic duties. He will "help out whenever he can" around the house. He watches television, listens to his stereo and watches videos to "kill time". He has a computer at home but tends to use the Job Club facilities if he needs to work on resumés. Bruno has only been unemployed for a short period and says his main incentive for "going straight into the Job Club" was to avoid slipping into watching too much television. Being at the Job Club means he does not have to "kill time" at the family home. His activities outside the home have not been particularly affected. Aside from finding that he cannot afford to socialise with friends as much as he would like, his outside activities have not been affected because he was not involved in sports prior to unemployment. He identified "driving around" as a leisure activity he can no longer do due to the cost of fuel ("I really loved driving around, I can't do that as much as I used to").

For inner resources and skills Bruno identifies motivation as a trait. He reports being "pretty motivated" to find a position. He considers himself to be "a bit shy" but thinks he has good people skills. He sees his family as an external resource, both from practical and emotional standpoints. Friends are also a support. They will drive Bruno to job interviews if he does not have transport. Bruno says he feels his self-esteem has "dropped a bit" due to the process of searching and not being successful, but he is positive that if he keeps going he will be successful.

Walter, aged 25

When Walter lost his job he was "worried and anxious" about his financial position. He also initially felt "rejected" not fully understanding why he had been let go. This feeling only lasted a short period of time. His self-confidence was adversely affected.

Walter's job search included asking "a lot of my mates because they are working" for a position. He also goes to the CES to read the notice boards. Initially he did not send out letters or resumés, preferring to only apply for positions that were advertised as vacant. It is only recently that Walter has expanded his job search strategies to include these methods. The Job Club has provided him with the facilities and help to do this. The frustrations he encountered in searching for a job included what he perceived to be "prejudice" because of his criminal record. He feels employers are not willing to give him a chance. Walter also reports various practical frustrations including not being able to afford petrol for his car as well as the cost of public transport. He says "it's pretty hard. The dole does not give you enough money..." Walter's clothes are no longer suitable for job interviews and he cannot afford to buy new ones. This affects his confidence in interviews.

Walter would "rather be working" than be bored with unemployment. Three months before the interview he "sort of went through a stage where I didn't really care for a while". He was not motivated to seek employment. Presently he reports searching for work much more keenly. Working would provide him with financial stability as well as a daily structure.

A reduced income means "you don't go out. That's about it". Walter reports he is not able to budget and his money is usually gone in the "first five days (of the allowance period)". His income means he cannot "get all the things he wants" (he gives an example of a pair of shoes costing approximately half of his two weekly unemployment allowance). Walter tends not to go out on weekends due to the cost. He does not see friends as much as he did when employed.

Walter lives by himself and says his situation has no effect on his family. He visits his father on the weekends and considers him to be supportive and understanding of the difficulties associated with job search. His father lives locally so transport costs are not an issue.

Walter's activities at home include "a lot more television" and videos. He says he is very bored at home and simply tries to "sleep to kill time". He will take afternoon naps for "a few hours". Walter will also occasionally do gardening. Activities out side of the home have been affected in certain areas but not others. Whereas he cannot afford to "go out" as much, his major leisure activities appear not to have been affected. Walter reports "living at the beach". He will fish, skin dive, walk or swim. All of these leisure activities are very cheap because he uses the beach as the basis for all activities. Walter did not have any sporting commitments prior to unemployment.

When asked about inner resources Walter says he is "tolerant". He can "wait a lot longer for things to come along". Walter considers initially he was negative about his situation and the process of obtaining a new position. His attitude has changed to one of being patient and positive. Walter wants employment not only for the financial stability but also in order to raise his "self-esteem". He feels that he is more self confident when working and feels better about himself. His external resources include the Job Club and friends who "help me out a lot". They give Walter casual work as well as lending him money when he is in difficulty. He knows his father is supportive and would offer financial assistance, but he does not want to ask his father for money at this stage.

Walter says that not having full-time employment has meant he has "lost interest in most things". He has little motivation to "get up and go" (to find new interests, hobbies etc.). He feels that working would make him appreciate free time much more and motivate him to use such time "more wisely".

Simon, aged 29

Simon simply felt "annoyed" when he lost his last position. This soon became anger as he began worrying about money problems and his future. He is now "being used to it (unemployment)". Simon is feeling confident because recently he had a series of interviews. Three months previous to this Simon was "very negative" about his situation and prospects. He was "basically depressed". This depression manifested itself in the form of a lack of motivation to search for a new position and he "... couldn't be bothered doing anything. Didn't really care about anything". Simon says he now has more of a goal and this has helped him become motivated again.

Simon has taken the usual steps to find work. He has "sent out lots of letters", made phone calls, CES, newspapers and "just asking people". He reports "doing everything you can do". Simon has also used the internet. The biggest hurdle he currently faces is not having his driver's licence. He finds public transport inadequate and employers require a licence before they will employ him. A prospective employer told him that if he had a driver's licence he would have been successful in obtaining the position.

Simon reports seeking full-time employment more keenly than previously. He says he was "half-hearted" initially but is now "fed up with being unemployed" and is actively seeking work.

A reduced income has affected upon Simon's lifestyle. He "cuts back on lots of things like going out, spending". He has a cheque overdraft at the bank to cover any shortfall. He says entertainment suffers in particular. He will go out "a lot less" and simply visit friends more often. Simon also reports not "purchasing things for myself". It is also difficult for him to support his smoking habit. He presently lives at the family home as a way of coping with unemployment. He does not have a "regular social life" due to financial difficulties. He also had his car repossessed because he was unable to make the repayments. Training for a private pilot's license has also ceased until he has a regular income to afford lessons again.

Unemployment did not have a great impact upon Simon's family. He reports that they "basically have their own lives" but are fairly supportive on the whole. There was a time when they were 'naggy' but they tend to leave him alone at present. They want him to find full-time work. His relationships with friends have suffered, "socially I'm dead. I didn't think it could get any deader", due to lack of transport and money to participate in activities with friends.

Simon says that he has been at home much more since becoming unemployed. He spends a great deal of time on his computer, both for entertainment as well as updating his resumé and writing letters. Simon "hardly ever watches television" but reads quite often. He is currently studying the theory side of his pilot's licence in order to be ready for the practical side when he can afford to fly again. Simon does not like gardening but will do odd jobs around the home.

Simon's leisure activities outside of the home tend to include cheaper forms of recreation. He reports "just walking on the beach. Just walking to pass the time". He will listen to his walkman when on the beach. Simon's social life in general suffered because he was unable to afford to go to pubs/nightclubs with friends. He did not participate in general sports before unemployment and so has not had to give up any commitments. Simon can no longer plan to travel due to his circumstances. This is a particular disappointment.

In terms of inner strengths, Simon lists persistence as a positive trait. He believes that "a lot of people just stop and that's it". Since participating in the Job Club he has also become more motivated being with people in the same circumstances as himself and seeing how positive they are. He also says he is happier with his "people skills" since participating in the Job Club programs. Others completing the program provide him with ideas about a way of "doing things". His external resources include the Job Club, CES and family/friends.

Rodger, aged 24

Rodger was confused about "what to do next" when he was told he had lost his position. He was initially "a little anxious" about his future, but currently is less anxious and stressed than he was three months previously.

Rodger's job search included "doing a course" to improve his education and training. Upon completion of this course he joined the Job Club, primarily to understand "how to apply for work" rather than improve his skills base. He currently uses the newspaper, makes phone calls from the Job Club, uses the CES facilities and sends out resumés on a cold canvass basis. At present he feels frustrated and "annoyed" that he is "doing his best" at interviews and applying for positions but is not successful. Being turned down for a position he "really wants" makes Rodger feel he is not making any progress. At present he lives with his parents and has some savings. At this stage he reports that the more practical frustrations, such as the cost of fuel, have had no impact on his job search.

Participating in the Job Club has made him more "enthusiastic" to search for work. He now feels "less cautious" about whom he applies to for positions. The Job Club has provided him with a series of skills and opportunities to contact potential employers. He is "much more motivated" at present. Other results of unemployment such as boredom and "desperation" have also played a part in Rodgers increased search for employment.

Reduced income is a difficulty. Rodger reports "only going to the bank once a week" and spending only the amount he has in his wallet. He spends much more time with the Scouts organization because the involvement is not too expensive. When he participates in activities with the organization the cost of entrance to venues and transport is borne by the Scouts. When buying food he will "think twice" about purchasing the item, whereas before unemployment he would simply buy what he saw. Rodger will spend more time "shopping for bargains". He says he has not bought "luxury items", such as CDs, "for a long time while I've been unemployed".

Rodger lives at home. Becoming unemployed created difficulties for his family. He says they became "a little frustrated" with his situation. They tried to be as supportive as they could by providing "motivation", helping him look through the paper – often pointing out positions he was not qualified to apply for. At times they became "uptight", resulting in what Rodger calls "discussions". At first he considered his family did not fully appreciate his situation. He feels they now have more of an understanding about the difficulties of job search.

Rodger's out-of-home activities have also been affected upon. He has had to give up canoeing as a sporting activity due to the cost of transport and equipment. He is more selective in the activities for entertainment he will choose. He feels in general he is "restricted" with regard to how far he can travel to a venue and how long he can afford to stay. He now tends to look for venues closer to home. Rodger thinks he goes out less for meals than he did when employed.

Rodger's activities at home include more house work than previously. He will tend to help with the domestic duties whereas before he "tended to leave them to mum". With regard to entertainment he reports "the same amount of reading or TV ... as I did before".

When asked about inner resources and strengths, Rodger feels he is 'patient'. He is confident and happy that "something will eventually come along". He reports being very motivated. Being involved with the Scouts helps him "take his mind of things". His other external resources include family and friends, his family in particular will help him financially by allowing him to pay rent when he can.

Justin, aged 20

When Justin first lost his position he was not particularly concerned. He reports the loss as "no big deal" because he was not really enjoying the job. However, Justin concedes that he "felt lost" due to not having another job to go to. After a period of time, financial difficulties also became a concern. He began considering his future. He became anxious about his "future direction". The lack of direction affected his motivation to search for a position. Presently Justin says he is "not fazed about unemployment", but he is willing to wait for a position he will "really enjoy". He thinks he is over "the initial shock of not having work".

The Job Club has been Justin's main strategy in securing a full-time position. It has allowed him to "network". He also relies on "word of mouth" with friends to secure work, usually on a casual basis. Justin says he goes through the usual "bullshit" of phoning potential employers, using the CES and newspapers. A particular frustration for Justin was having to "chop of his hair" in order to increase what he perceived to be his chances of obtaining employment. He resents having to dramatically change his appearance. There was also the difficulty of employers wanting experience and skills which Justin did not possess.

At present Justin reports seeking work more keenly than when he first lost his position. He considers his efforts have increased "ten fold, heaps, heaps more". The main reasons for this are the closeness of the Christmas period and his wish to afford to travel in the future.

Justin identifies public transport as a strategy for dealing with a reduced income. He utilises the concession cards provided by Social Security. He reports "I don't drive much. I don't eat as well as I should. I'm living of rice and pastas mostly". He will not rent videos or buy new books. He has "just cut back on everything". Other impacts of unemployment include not "planning to do things" due to not being able to save for future events, and only spending on the "necessities of life" (he gives the example of going to the laundromat). Justin has cut back on entertainment because the cost of driving and the price of admission to venues. He moved back to the family home after being unemployed.

Justin's situation caused a degree of "stress" to his family. He reports "it was a lot more stress on them than it was for me". He feels their stress was the result of them seeing that "their son was not having an enjoyable life, not being able to have all the things he wanted". Justin considers they were supportive but "not 100%", their ideas of suitable positions differed somewhat from his and this caused arguments on occasions.

Justin says he enjoys photography and artwork as home based activities. Unemployment has meant not being able to pursue these activities because of the cost of buying paints, brushes and photographic film: "I have the time now, but not the money". Justin does more gardening and listens to music, "stuff that doesn't cost anything". He tends not to watch television.

Unemployment has had a "detrimental effect" on Justin's activities outside of the home. He will tend to get involved in free activities such as walking on the beach. He finds that "everything costs money". Justin says that even going to the park or beach costs money because becoming thirsty means buying a drink. He cannot go to the "pub for a middy with his mates" or out to dinner.

Justin identifies his ability "not to get down" as an inner strength. He says he is pretty positive about "stuff". He also considers himself to be "emotionally balanced", commenting that it is pointless getting upset about not having work. Justin relies on meditation to keep from going "nuts" about being unemployed. His external resources include family and friends. Friends provide him with casual work as well as information concerning potential full-time opportunities. Justin's family is supportive and have on occasions helped him prepare letters and resumés for positions. He considers that they are a potential financial support but at this stage he does not want "to use them".

Gordon, aged 22

Gordon was "extremely disappointed" when informed he had lost his position. It was particularly disappointing as it was a paid trainee position with specific duties within the company. He was not sure "who to get angry at" for the loss of full-time work. Gordon said he was frustrated at having to "jump back into job search" and "annoyed" that the position he lost was one which he was interested in pursuing as a career.

Gordon has relied heavily on cold canvassing as a method of securing work. He will present his resumé in person to the businesses he would like to work for. The CES and Job Club services provide him with the resources to write letters to potential employers and up-date his resumé. Gordon believes he has done "pretty much everything" to secure a position. In terms of the frustrations of job search he identifies the "constant non-replies" as annoying. He considers it frustrating that he puts so much effort into applying for jobs and many employers simply do not show the common courtesy to contact him regarding whether or not he was successful.

Gordon finds the whole job search process frustrating. "It's like a vicious circle... sitting at home ...you are not earning money". A more practical frustration is the reliance on public transport, "... having to catch three buses, then a train. That costs money". At one point he relied on a pushbike for transport due to the cost of running a car. Gordon reports seeking employment more keenly than three months before. He is in the "mode" of getting up and searching as opposed to the "mode" of sleeping in and being lazy.

A reduced income is "not really a problem". Gordon says he is "good at going without things". He will cut back on "week-end drinks". Having a budget has also helped. His priorities are food, clothes then sports' fees. Gordon will buy the "best brand at the cheapest price" when shopping. The main constraint he identified was "not going out with mates". He will spend $20 a weekend on entertainment at home rather than $50 on one night out.

Gordon's family is supportive. They will not charge him board when he is unemployed. When he has work he will contribute "a bit more" than just board. He concedes that on occasion frustrations about his situation are taken out on his family, but they understand what he is going through and are supportive ("they've been really good").

Gordon's activities at home have been affected in a "positive" way. His major leisure activity is creating and producing music. Unemployment has given him more time to do this on equipment he already owns. He will use his computer and occasionally read. Gordon doesn't watch more television than he did previously. His out-of-home leisure includes shooting basketball in the park and still participating in team sports (basketball). At present Gordon has not given up sporting commitments. He has however had to reduce "going out to bars" due to the cost. He will now tend to go around to friends' houses for entertainment.

When asked about inner resources and skills, Gordon says he is positive about his future, "just knowing I have the skills to get a job'. He is basically a "happy" person who will not let situations get him down. Gordon will not let himself become "depressed" because he feels this will effect his ability to present well in job interviews. He feels a positive frame of mind is important.

Gordon's external resources include his family who are "always there". He considers some of his friends are "unsupportive", they are "a bit sick of me not having a job". Other friends are more supportive and will often look for positions for him. He identifies the Job Club as a support because it provides him with resources to apply for positions ("saves me $10 in letters each week").

Gordon considers being unemployed has affected his goals. He cannot plan to travel or pursue his career which is music. "You need a career and you need to be earning money to be able to survive. There's a lot of enjoyment taken away knowing you're not getting anywhere". He misses the interactions with people that a full-time position provides.

Wayne, aged 21

Wayne reported not being "overly concerned" when told he had lost his position. He was optimistic that his period of unemployment would be a short one. As time progressed he "became a bit more pessimistic when you realise that there aren't any job opportunities there, but at the time I didn't consider that it would be a major problem". Wayne finds it "annoying" not having full-time employment. He would like "something to actually do during the day". He misses the structure a full-time position provides.

Wayne has been "doing as much as I can to help my chances" in terms of job search. He has attended the Job Club and checks the CES notice boards. Wayne also relies on word-of-mouth from friends to inform him of available work. His other strategies include cold canvassing, newspapers and the Internet. His main frustration in searching for a job has been the constant "knock backs", "you feel like you are getting close...then someone pips you at the post". Wayne reports seeking work more keenly than three months previously. He identifies the risk of being identified as "long term unemployed" as his motivation for searching more keenly. He says "the longer you go (search) the more desperate you get".

A reduced income simply means "buying less things". An identified problem is an inability to save. Wayne cannot put money aside for a car or simply to "get anywhere". He will spend less when he goes out on weekends. He finds it a frustration not being able to pay for his girlfriend when they go out. Wayne has not had to give up any sporting commitments because of reduced income. He still participates in his Judo club, but he cannot do "expensive things".

Wayne is "not sure" what effect his situation has had on his family. He feels they know he will be successful in obtaining a position eventually. He considers both his family and girlfriend have been supportive.

Wayne's activities at home were not overly affected. He reports reading "quite a bit more" than prior to unemployment but no real increase in watching television. His activities outside of the home have not been affected, "I can't honestly say that it's affected my activities outside of the home" (earlier in the interview he reported not being able to "go out" as much).

When asked about inner strengths, Wayne says he considers that "I suppose I just keep on going. A lot of people give up" (a positive attitude). Wayne uses the words "positive" and "determined" to describe himself. He also considers his "perseverance" is a particular trait. He does not get "down or depressed". He identifies his family as well as his girlfriend as external resources in as much as they are supportive ("I rely on them for support..."). Wayne believes "leisure activities ... tend to divert my thoughts away from being negative or focusing to much on not having a job". Friends provide leads to potential positions as well as an avenue to casual work.

A summary of the impact on the eight categories of the unemployment experience is listed in Table 6.2. In the following section, each category of experience is analysed on a gender basis.

Analysis of the Categories of Experience

The eight categories of experience, which include unemployment impact, job search, reduced income, family relationships/responsibilities, activities at home, out-of-home activities, personal and external resources will be analysed between males and females. Differences and similarities will be noted as to how experience of job loss is affected by gender.

Unemployment Impact

Responses to the impact of unemployment may be put into several categories: being demoralised and depressed; angry, upset and anxious; financially insecure; structure of work missed; positive over time; and unconcern replaced by desperation. The frequencies are included in Table 6.3.

Table 6.3
Unemployment Impact

Impact groupings	Females	Males
Angry/upset/anxious	4	7
Positive over time	5	3
Financially insecure	2	5
Depressed/demoralised	5	1
Structure of work missed	3	2
Unconcern replaced by desperation	-	4

Unemployment impacted badly on young females. At least five said that unemployment made them depressed and demoralised. Four others said they were angry, upset and anxious. Loss of financial security was mentioned by two and three others missed the routine and structure of work. One woman felt disappointed. The initial depression, disappointment, anger and anxiety did not persist over time, as five said that they were more positive at the time the interviews were conducted. The worst case of adverse impact was the suicidal tendency of one female, which was only relieved by the birth of her daughter. For another illness followed to ameliorate the unemployed role.

Unemployment impacted adversely on men as well. Five males were concerned about financial difficulties as compared to two females. Seven expressed anger, anxiety and disappointment, but only one felt depressed. Two expressed problems about planning for the future. For four men unemployment caused little concern, but as the length of unemployment increased, they were getting desperate. Three felt more positive over time.

The data in Table 6.3 suggest that more women than men tended to be depressed and demoralised than men as a result of job loss. More men felt angry, upset and anxious and financially insecure than women. Men who are optimistic about future employment soon after losing their job, get desperate as the length of unemployment increases. Both sexes missed the structure of work and felt positive over time and after initial trauma experienced after losing their job.

Job Search

The effects of job search were felt in several ways. Six major groupings were devised. The included: acquisition of skills at job club; multi-method search; lack of transport; interview clothing; lack of qualification/experience; and frustration of rejection. Frequencies of these groupings are in Table 6.4.

Table 6.4
Job Search Impact

Job search groupings	Females	Males
Acquisition of skills at job club	7	8
Multi-method search	7	7
Lack of qualifications/experience	5	2
Frustration of rejections	2	4
Interview clothing	3	2
Lack of transport	2	1

For all males and females the search was painful and frustrating. The majority (7 females and 8 males) found that skills acquired at the Job Club were very useful. Fourteen of the 20 interviewed (7 females, 7 males) used various methods of job search. These included: telephoning; writing letters; using the facsimile machine; work-of-mouth contacts; and cold canvassing. At the Job Club, individuals were able to develop their resumés and use communication resources which were made available. The major problems in acquiring jobs were the lack of qualifications and experience (females 5; males 2). Persistent rejections and at times the lack of acknowledgment caused frustrations (females 2; males 4). Other constraints which affected job search were the lack of transport (females 3; males 2) and inadequate interview clothing (females 2; males 1). Two males who used cold canvassing as their only job search method. One female found work experience stressful and another ameliorated job loss by doing volunteer work. For one male, language difficulties hampered the job search process.

Reduced Income

Lack of an adequate income resulted in several deprivations, such as acquiring second-hand clothing, cheaper food, difficulties in meeting bills, tighter budgets, less socialising and entertainment and just staying at home. Frequencies of these deprivations are shown in Table 6.5

The lack of income caused jobless young people to restrict a number of their customary activities. Seven females and three males had to buy cheaper food and six males and four females could not buy new clothes or had to buy second-hand apparel. Socialising and entertainment were also curtailed for seven females and six males. Five females said they had difficulties paying bills and both sexes reported having to devise a tight budget (females 3; males 2). Four males found surviving on their own difficult and had to move back to the family home. Three females were confined to activities at home because of the lack of income.

Table 6.5
Impact of Reduced Income

Reduced income groupings	Females	Males
Angry/upset/anxious	7	3
Acquiring second-hand clothes	4	6
Less socialising entertainment	5	3
Difficulties paying bills	5	-
Budget tightening	3	2
Staying at home	3	-

Family Relationships/Responsibilities

A variety of responses were given to questions on family relationships and responsibilities. These were grouped under the following headings: family supportive; anxiety of parents; perceived as not trying; and adoption of household roles. The frequencies are in Table 6.6.

All men interviewed said that their families were supportive, but only five females reported such relationships. These relationships were mainly with parents, but grandparents and boy friends (in the case of females) and friends also played a role in supporting relationships. In saying that relationships were generally positive, there were reports of parents' anxiety and strains as the unemployment experience lengthened (females 4; males 5). Three females said that they were seen to be not trying for work. A small number (2 females; 1 male) took on more household roles. Financial support for one female was not without friction with the parent. For another being at home and sullen was seen negatively by the parent and yet another female tended to isolate herself in her room to avoid arguments. The employment of siblings was the cause of envy for one female.

Table 6.6
Family Relationships and Responsibilities

Relationships/Responsibilities	Females	Males
Family/friends supportive	5	10
Parental anxiety	4	5
Perceived as not trying	3	-
Adoption of household roles	2	1

Activities at Home

Young people participated in a number of activities in the home during unemployment. Electronic activities, gardening, television viewing, domestic chores, and reading were dominant activities in the home. The frequencies are listed in Table 6.7.

Table 6.7
Activities at Home

Activities at home	Females	Males
Electronic activities	8	4
Domestic chores	7	4
More reading	6	2
More TV/videos	4	3
Less TV/videos	3	3
Gardening	1	4

The use of electronics was dominant among females (8) and frequent among males (4). The computer, telephone, radio and hi-fi were used to fill time and for females to keep in touch with their friends especially through the use of the phone. Females (7) tended to get involved in household chores more than males (4), but more males (4) than females (1) worked in the garden. Some watched more television (4 females; 3 males) and others less (females 3; males 3). Females (6) tended to read more than males (2) and two females said that they now met their friends at home. It appeared that females were more involved in household chores of cleaning and cooking and males in doing things with their hands, which required repairing and fixing skills. One male decided to give up his hobby of photography as a hobby because of the lack of money.

Out-of-Home Activities

Out-of-home activities were affected by unemployment. The responses included cheaper forms of activity, less sporting activity, social discomfort, less commercial recreation and going out less. The frequencies are in Table 6.8.

Table 6.8
Out-of-Home Activities

Out-of-home activities	Females	Males
Cheaper forms	4	7
Social discomfort	4	3
Less sporting activities	6	-
Going out less	3	3
Less commercial recreation	2	4

A large proportion of young people participated in cheaper forms of recreation (males 7; females 4). These included activities such as walking, jogging, cycling and visits to parks. Six females curtailed sporting activities because of membership and transport costs. Only two males reported being involved in organised sport before losing their job and these activities continued in unemployment. Males and females (3 each) went out less, and expressed concerns of social discomfort in the company of others (4 females; 3 males). Commercial activities meant visiting pubs, nightclubs, going to movies and in one case visiting go-karting and pot black venues. One female said she attended cheaper parties as a substitute for other forms of commercial recreation.

Personal Resources

Responses of the young people on their personal resources revealed that they remained positive and motivated, but setbacks cause mood swings (Table 6.9).

Table 6.9
Personal Resources

Personal resources	Females	Males
Positive & motivated	10	10
Mood swings	4	2
Independent	2	-

All the young people interviewed felt that their personal resources were the positive feelings that they had about themselves and motivation levels were still high. Some admitted that they were affected by mood swings. High motivation levels were affected by job rejections, which sometimes led to feeling "down" and "depressed". Four females and two males reported feeling that way. However, responses of wanting to be independent, keep busy and persisting were personal attributes which some made a point to mention.

External Resources

Employment and job training agencies and friends and family were the main external resources (Table 6.10).

Table 6.10
External Resources

External resources	Females	Males
Family & friends	10	10
Employment/job training agencies	8	10

All Job Club participants were interviewed at Job Club venues. They were appreciative of the practical help they received and the resources that were available to them. They also felt that employment agencies were helpful. These practical supports were aided by emotional and financial support by family and friends. Although social discomfort with friends was mentioned earlier, close support was often given by many friends and those close to the participants like boy- and girl-friends.

Data in this chapter reveal how young unemployed people cope with the eight categories of experience. Deprivations arising out of job loss affect customary lifestyle patterns. Those unable to cope find their mental and physical health adversely affected. Some experiences of deprivation may be ameliorated by the provision of public recreation services. The problem of providing such services to the unemployed is the subject of a later chapter.

7

Employment Benefits and Losses

A subsidiary sample of young people was used to study the question of benefits and losses of employment (see Chapter 3). The 44 participants in the study were asked two questions about employment. First. "When your were in employment, what were the benefits your gained?" Second, "When you were in employment, what were some of your losses?" Thirty eight participants responded to the question and all said that the gains were "money" and the losses were "less time". (Six participants either did not answer the question or their responses could not be deciphered). All of the 38 respondents expanded on their answers as to how and why money and time affected their leisure. Patrick, aged 30, showed how money paid for his leisure, but he had less time to participate.

> *Employment benefit*: Leisure, recreation ... There was money, always had money to go out and pay for leisure and recreation activities, socialising, you had a bit more a life than what you would otherwise. Yeah, yes, cause you usually lead two lives, you lead your one at home and you lead the other one when you are at your work place because you spend most of your time at work than what you do at home.

Employment loss: Not enough time to do them, yeah not enough time to do certain leisure activities, getting up in the morning, that was a restraint. Yeah, it usually works out easy, you work flat out all the time and you've got lots of money or you work hardly at all and you have no money.

For Kathleen, aged 29, money meant more self-esteem, but loss of quality time to spend with friends:

Employment benefit: More money to spend on those things. A greater sense of self-esteem. Therefore I wanted to leave the house and participate in those things.

Employment loss: Loss of time. Unable to join my friends who were students. Basically most of my time spent working and I'm too tired to go out after. Yes that is it, loss of quality time.

Brigette, age 28, spoke of freedom, peace of mind and a decent social life in employment with a 9 to 5 job:

Employment benefit: Being able to go out at night time and go shopping on a Saturday. Not having to worry about money all the time. Freedom of movement in all respects. It's just freedom, peace of mind. Just being able to do things, you have a decent social life.

Employment loss: Well in my particular situation I had a very stable 9 - 5 situation so my actual employment at the time doesn't really impede on anything, you know. Like I never had to do overtime. Most of my friends worked and went to college at the same time, so it wasn't as if I was missing out on anything during working hours.

The overwhelming conclusion from these accounts is that employment brings monetary benefits, but people may have less time to participate in leisure activities. The three examples show that money enables leisure participation and a decent social life, enhances self-esteem and gives a sense of freedom and peace of mind.

Home-based Activities

Study participants were asked about the activities they did in the home before and after unemployment. Six major activities were mentioned, but there were several others that had frequencies of less than two. The major activities are listed in Table 7.1.

Table 7.1
Activities at Home

Activities at home	Before job loss	After job loss	
		Continued	*Discontinued*
TV/Videos	42	42	0
Computer Activities	16	16	0
Gardening	12	12	0
Art Craft Hobbies	5	5	0
Reading	27	27	0
Listening to Music	23	23	0
Total	125	125	0

The other activities mentioned included: guitar playing ; remote control cars; cooking (2); drinking; cleaning house; more socialising; crosswords; playing flute; walk the dog; yoga; darts/cards; writing music; general exercises; playing pool (1).

Table 7.1 shows that activities participated in before unemployment continued after job loss. However, in unemployment there were those who participated less, some more and others did activities just to fill time. Jimmy, aged 18, was involved in a number of activities before unemployment, but his guitar playing increased after he lost his job:

Before: Playing guitar, playing the computer, listening to music.

After: Probably more. Specifically I play the guitar more; I started writing music a lot more and stuff like that. More television viewing, but computer usage is about the same.

Margaret, aged 30, did a lot more cleaning to kill time, but read a lot more:

Before: Read. Read books, do nothing, watch TV, watch videos, gardening, veggies and stuff.

After: I did more cleaning. It is not a leisure time activity. It became a killer of time. Probably more reading, I became a member of the local library and got books out. More socialising ... I was bored after a whole day doing nothing or being on my own.

Nicola, aged 23, spent a lot of time thinking about job search and reemployment, but she also had motivation problems:

Before: When I came home from work I would just veg in front of the television, just to relax and find something to eat. So on the weekends I would catch up with friends, there would be more socialising.

After: I know it sounds a bit strange, but you sort of had to sit down and think of ways to get out of being unemployed, 'cause I don't want to be, so that sort of took a lot of my time, and getting a lot of things organised, and dates, taking priority ...but motivation is hard one to come by as well. When you don't have the motivation to go out and do something, then TV is free to sit down and relax.

Claudia, aged 28, did a lot more of her pre-unemployment activities because they were cheap:

Before: Reading is one of my big ones. Cooking, gardening. I do quite a bit of yoga. Sometimes TV, but not really a hell of a lot.

After: I did probably more of these activities because it is cheap entertainment. I could quite easily cook for a whole week on end. I like reading for my own enjoyment, not reading for study. That's probably one of the big things I really picked on.

Christina, aged 28, did less in the home. She felt unmotivated and found her hobbies unaffordable:

Before: TV, watching videos. I don't know, sometimes I'd like to get more craft things together, could be anything like just doing a bit of painting, or a bit of sketching, because when I was working I felt like I was more motivated to do things.

After: I actually done less, believe it or not! I think I have lost motivation ... the fact is you have to spend money on these things, get the paint and buy bits and pieces. You have this thing about money – which puts you off splurging ...and also the motivation goes. You're trapped. More TV, I am sure I do more of that ...same amount of reading.

These comments suggest that young people who are involved with home activities before job loss continue with their activities in unemployment. However, the main reason for continuing with was to fill time. Some participated less and felt unmotivated to be fully involved in home activities. Others continued with activities because they were cheap. The few who increased participation were able to do so because they had the time and did not feel guilty about doing activities they were accustomed to before unemployment. Except for the last example, unemployment seemed to affect activities in the home. The quality of the leisure experience was diminished either by 'filling time', or by the lack of motivation to be engaged in an activity. Cost also was an impediment that allowed cheap activities to continue.

Fitness Activities

Questions were asked about fitness activities participated in before and after unemployment. All participants responded to the question, but seven indicated that they did nothing. Eight major categories of fitness activities were mentioned. They included: organised sport, swimming, jogging, walking, gym, bike riding, walk the dog, and martial arts. The frequencies are presented in Table 7. 2.

Table 7.2
Activities for Fitness

Fitness Activities	Before job loss	After job loss	
		Continued	Discontinued
Organised Sport	23	9	14
Swimming	10	4	6
Jogging	9	5	4
Walking	9	8	1
Gym	8	2	6
Bike riding	4	3	1
Walk the dog	3	3	0
Martial arts	2	2	0
Total	68	36	32

The participants indicated several activities that were included under organised sport: They were: football (6); basketball (4); cricket, netball (3); soccer, golf (2); rugby, horseriding, tennis, rollerblading, squash, sailing, yoga, water skiing, rowing, fishing, and volleyball (1).

The cluster of eight fitness activities was mentioned 68 times before job loss. However, after unemployment 36 activities were continued and 32 discontinued. The major reason for withdrawal was the cost of participating. Low cost activities like walking, bike riding, walking the dog and martial arts were not often stopped. But the higher cost activities of organised sport, swimming, and gym were more often given up. There is no explanation why the low cost activity of jogging had a high withdrawal rate, but it could well be due to the lack of motivation rather than cost. Cheap activity and more time meant that Margaret, aged 30 could spend more time at the beach:

Before: Going to the beach – swimming, walking. Well I had more time to do stuff like to go to the beach and to walk further because I used to go to the beach and walk or ride and do my exercises before work, so I'd have to get up early to do that.

After: But when I was unemployed I could actually take my time get down there at nine stay till mid day. I did more exercise that was free. I had more time to do it, so that's how it was affected. I increased these activities when I was unemployed, because I could. But there were the free ones, not like aerobics. But they were generally my activities anyway.

Lyle, aged 24, had to give up expensive activities, but continued with cheaper ones:

Before: For fitness I did jujitsu and football. That's for team sport. But I enjoyed doing other sports. I just generally enjoy doing sports all the time. I wasn't able to afford doing football. Like cricket I just go down to the nets with a couple of mates and hit a ball about – so I can do that in my leisure time with no money involved.

After: Jujitsu I just couldn't afford it that would have been the reason I gave it up. That one and football but I will go down to the nets and play cricket which is free.

Thomas, aged 27, could not afford entry fees or travel costs, so his activities ceased:

Before: Surfing, swimming, jogging. I paid to go to the gym.

After: I had to give up swimming. I'd swim for a team and have to pay fees. Couldn't go travelling to go surfing because I couldn't afford fuel or sports shoes for jogging.

Gym membership for Greg, aged 24, was for him so expensive that he could not afford to attend sessions:

Before: Played touch rugby, a lot of sport bits and pieces, once a week or twice a week.

After: Well, I'd like to be a lot fitter but you just can't afford to go to the gym. I'd like to got to the gym once a day, but you just can't afford to. For membership at any gym it's going to cost you $300 for a year for starters.

From the responses of Margaret, Lyle, Thomas and Greg, it is quite clear that unemployment was an impediment to continuing customary fitness activities. In the case of Margaret, she could not afford aerobics, but more unobligated time enabled her to spend more time at the beach at times more convenient to her and it was free. In this instance, it could be said that job loss was a catalyst for more activities.

Social and Entertainment Activities

Questions about social and entertainment activities before and after unemployment elicited responses of: being with friends; pubs parties and dinners; recreation activities with friends; movies, nightclubs, discos and theatre. The frequencies before and after unemployment are in Table 7.3.

Table 7.3
Social and Entertainment Activities

Social/Entertainment Activities	Before job loss	After job loss	
		Continued	Discontinued
Being with friends	26	17	9
Pubs parties dinners	36	28	8
Recreation activities with friends	20	14	6
Movies, nightclubs, discos, theatre	28	14	14
Total	110	73	37

As a consequence of unemployment, several social and entertainment activities were affected: going to pubs ceased or decreased (18); being with friends including those from work ceased (9); there was an increase in visiting (4); cheaper venues were sought (2); eating out decreased; recreation with friends stopped; mixing with unemployed friends increased; and social stigma was experienced (1).

With social and entertainment activities, money played a big part in participation. Many discontinued participation and those who did continue with activities did so with much less frequency. Ron, aged 18, felt the loss of pride when he could not reciprocate buying his friends a drink at the pub:

> *Before*: Go out drinking with my mates to pubs and clubs, going bowling for a bit of a laugh sometimes.

> *After*: There's been a decrease in my participation. Bowling is pretty expensive anyway. And not being able to buy your rounds is a big thing. I suppose it's a pride thing.

For Genevieve, aged 28, socialising with friends decreased, as did going to pubs and clubs:

> *Before*: Going out with friends. They would come here or I would go to their places. Out to dinner, out to pubs, clubs, movies with friends.

> *After*: Not so much at the moment. There has been a decrease going out to pubs clubs. I just don't feel like it at the moment actually. Money does play a part. I wouldn't be able to do it as often.

Brendon, aged 27, who was a committed art lover, still went to shows after he lost his job, but made use of concession entry:

> *Before*: I go to see plays and stuff. movies. You know like art. I think art is entertainment – so art shows either performance or visual art. I suppose I get a social benefit. I get to meet new people and I get an intellectual benefit, as I actually get something out of it ... like an art show and I appreciate the art and I get something from that.

> *After*: I still go to art shows, still go to the movies, because being unemployed I get a discount so it's sort of like an incentive to

go. I've been to plays and stuff – like the theatre. I'd say a general increase. More time and I also get access to things that don't cost. I don't always go to the theatres and plays. Concessions - I seem to be more aware of things, and I'm more available for things that are free or whatever, so I take advantage of them because I have no excuse not to, in my mind.

Once again the findings on social and entertainment activities of young people indicate that lack of money is a major cause of reduced or non-participation in customary activities. Many young people discontinued their entertainment activities and also being with their friends. High frequency activities like pubs, parties and dinners were also affected by the lack of money. Unemployment was clearly an impediment to participation in desired social and entertainment leisure activities.

Conclusions

This research asked the question whether unemployment was an impediment or catalyst for leisure and human development. The data on home-based activities did not indicate discontinuity, but the quality of involvement was diminished because of the material and psychological deprivation. In the case of fitness and social and entertainment activities, the lack of money resulted in diminished and discontinued participation. So in Kelly's terms (1980), the losses far outweighed the gains. This applied especially to out-of-home activities. It must therefore be concluded that unemployment is for most an impediment to leisure and therefore, human development. For the few who cope with low cost activity, their personal agency (Fryer, 1995) must be commended.

8

Providers' Perceptions of Services to the Unemployed

This chapter on providers' perceptions of services to the unemployed is structured around seven variables. These include organisational policy, providers' philosophy, economic demands, contracting services, equity measures, unemployment programs and types of programs. Based on these variables profiles for local authorities of Wentworth, Shenton, Bradford, Melton, Cranston, Brinkley, Preston, Oakwood and Ravenswood are presented. The chapter concludes with a comparison of the nine local authorities on each of the variables discussed in the depth interviews.

Wentworth

Wentworth's policy and philosophy of leisure service provision and delivery is one of providing opportunities for participation for all sections of the community. This is achieved by direct service provision (swimming classes, fitness centres etc.) as well as providing facilities that are utilised by clubs and community organisations.

In general this policy/philosophy is consistent with the views of the interviewee. He sees a 'dynamic tension' between financial considerations and social responsibilities. A 'happy medium' needs to be found between the cost of providing a cross-section of leisure services and adhering to a service delivery model that does not simply put the dollar cost as the bottom line. The cost of providing a service to a particular section of the community has to be measured in terms of a financial cost and social cost, 'I don't necessarily believe that dollars are the whole ... be all and end all' was his remark.

Changes in the economic climate have 'absolutely' affected strategies for service delivery. Due to a policy of 'national competition' (providing a service at least as well as outside contractors or other local government authorities) the service has to be 'contestable'. However, he concedes that if there were a 'proven need' for a leisure service that would run at a consistent loss it would be considered a 'community benefit' and would be provided. This policy is essentially 'inconsistent' with the 'national competition' model.

Currently leisure services are not leased out to private contractors. However, strategies are being formulated to allow some services to be contracted out. Any service that is contracted out will only be leased to organizations whose philosophies of service delivery are 'consistent with those of the Shire'. The capital cost of providing the leisure facilities is an 'investment in the community' and that is the council's primary responsibility. Operating and building maintenance is a user pays issue. 'Community services is core business because those services should rightly be delivered ... but who actually runs aspects of those is a different issue entirely'. 'If a service is to be leased out the financial returns to the Council should be better than we're currently able to do ourselves' were the remarks of the provider.

How a contractor manages a service is not 'core business' for the Council. Which services are delivered is a concern for the Council. Delivery will primarily be 'dollar-driven' from a contractor's point of view, but existing users rights and needs must be protected. Any leased-out service must 'maximise returns', not necessarily dollar returns but providing a demanded service in such a way that the people in the immediate area of the community can participate. Ongoing evaluations of contractors would ensure they are 'performing to the standards and achieving the objectives we are looking for'.

Provisions are made for elements of the community to access leisure facilities. The Council does not charge 'juniors' for the use of facilities. Senior citizens are not charged for the use of senior citizen facilities. A range of concession cards is also available for 'people going to swimming pools and so on...'. Whereas there is a range of concessions for a variety of leisure services the concessions 'do not include unemployed people specifically'. The interviewee felt 'most definitely' that young unemployed people should be encouraged to lead healthy lifestyles, but demographic data show young unemployed people do not tend to use the facilities. There are no schemes in place to encourage greater participation from this group. Specific programs could be developed depending upon the provision of funding.

In keeping with the service delivery philosophy the interviewee concedes 'the unemployed need to have access to facilities and programs. It is a matter of structuring those programs in such a way that they are accessible to them both in a time sense and also from a financial point of view. Any program implemented for this segment of the community should stand on its own from a financial point of view. In practice there would be price structures, off-peak rates, no cost activities etc. All these would be considered 'where feasible'.

Formal research has been undertaken to identify young people in the region. The research was aimed at finding out which sectors of the community did not access leisure services and why. It will also help identify 'where young unemployed people are and what their issues are and what their recreational needs are so we can program to suit'. Such research is part of an overall strategy to ensure 'customer focus'.

The interviewee favours both special and mainstream programs for the young unemployed. The key to the provision is funding. If funding is available then there is 'no problem' with providing special programs specifically for the young unemployed, but in general they have access to the same mainstream programs as everyone else. There is a concern about 'isolating' young unemployed in specific programs. General integration is the preferred option. If the young unemployed were to be specifically targeted they would be catered for with regard to standard 'marketing philosophy', services would be tailored to meet their needs in terms of available time, cost considerations etc. Specific programs would be initially seen as a 'stepping-stone' to participation in mainstream services.

Other potential ideas for increasing the participation rates of the young unemployed include developing a 'primarily' youth-focused recreation centre (such as a youth service) but promoting access to more mainstream recreation such as sporting clubs and venues. A mix of both structured and unstructured programs would be available to maximise the potential of offering activities that would be utilised. A primary access point focusing on young people would ease the tensions of managing 'what young people want to do' compared to the rest of the community. Both structured and unstructured activities give young people the chance to simply socialise if that is their wish, or participate if that is what they want to do.

The interviewee concedes that delivery of leisure services to the young unemployed is 'fairly dismal'. The Council primarily runs structured programs and that does not always 'meet the needs of young people'. Success will come when delivery is less 'traditional' and more 'tailored' to them in terms of cost and their available time.

Shenton

The service delivery philosophy/policy of the City of Shenton is to 'plan, manage, coordinate and promote the provision of recreation facilities, services and resources in the City'. The overall philosophy is that the provision of these services is important to the quality of life of the people who live in the City of Shenton. Equity of access is important. Everybody should have access to activities, not just those who can afford to pay.

The philosophy/policy of the City of Shenton is consistent with the views/philosophy of the interviewee. Such services need to be provided at a local level. They need to be 'accessible services, in places where people live and work and so they have access to the spaces and also to the ... opportunities'.

Changes in the economic climate have 'very much' had an effect on the strategies of service delivery. National competition policy has had a particular effect - 'it has meant we are having to look at where we are competing with private enterprise, why we are competing'. There is now a need to effectively identify clearly what the community service obligations of the City are.

Aspects of leisure services are 'outsourced' to private enterprise. Contractors manage the services but the City still has a 'monitoring and supervisory role to make sure that they meet our quality expectations'. The objectives of the contractors are consistent with those of the City of Shenton. 'Profit is obviously the motive, but to meet that objective they need to get as many people in as they can'. The City derives benefit from this via having other services exposed to potential users by advertising at these venues as well as maximising the use of the provided facility. The City can also concentrate on providing 'more diverse programs that may be are not as profitable'. It would not be feasible to contract these services out due to the fact that contractors would not be able to run at a loss whereas the City would accept a financial loss as part of the provision of a community service.

Concessions are made for the 'disadvantaged segments' of the community. Government Health Care cards and concession cards are used as a test for discounted entry (this would presumably include the young unemployed if they had their unemployment cards). The City will also provide specific 'free events and activities' (fairs, carnivals, pageants and concerts) – 'an opportunity for the community to come together without a price tag on it'.

Young unemployed people should 'absolutely, full stop, end of story' be encouraged to lead a healthy lifestyle. This has 'positive aspects' for the community as a whole as it involves them in having contact with other community members. However, there are no programs in place specifically targeting the young unemployed. A program was in existence specifically targeting this group, but it was under-utilised and no longer exists.

The City is currently focusing on youth leisure having identified a need in this area, but there is no specific plan to target young unemployed people. It is anticipated that all young people will access certain leisure facilities when it is appropriate for them to do so. For example, a proposed skate board ramp would be accessible during the day by those youth who had the time to use it. Those areas defined as 'passive spaces' (parks and reserves) are also available to be utilised as individuals wish to. The more structured leisure services are accessible as part of the general strategy of concessions to the group, without targeting their patronage.

The City of Shenton is currently looking at 'partnership areas' to run pilot leisure programs for the young unemployed. The City will play a lead role in 'seed funding', but often the 'coordinating role is as much value as money'. If funding or partnerships could be found, the City may consider implementing programs specifically aimed at the young unemployed. There is presently no scheme in place to identify the number of young unemployed in the area. The use of a series of Federal Government concession cards at the various leisure services is an indication of which elements of the community are accessing which services. The interviewee concedes 'we are not counting heads as you go through, you're Aboriginal, are you unemployed ...'. The City will also use the Bureau of Statistics to identify and plan for specific groups. The previous program aimed at the young unemployed was based on a 'gut feeling' that such a program was needed in the area. A proposed 'survey on youth' to be carried out in the future will '...target young unemployed people ...as well'.

The City is 'keen to have some youth programs ...' but does not envisage special programs for the young unemployed as an individual group within the group of 'youth'. The interviewee feels that the young unemployed will be able to access such programs as part of the larger group of users. One reason for not wishing to focus specifically on the unemployed is that doing so would create 'false divisions' and a degree of labelling "you're unemployed therefore you can come and use the facility at this time" rather than, "I'd like to come and do things at the same time as my mates and be part of a larger group of people". He feels that such programs may not be well utilised due to 'labelling issues ... you know, if you're here between 9:00 and 3:00 it's obvious you're either a truant or unemployed, which has a stigma attached to it'. The benefits of involving them in mainstream programs include '...mingling with people..., they see other things happening, too'.

Any specific activities that are set up for the young unemployed would not 'run for ever and a day', they would be used as a 'come and try if it appeals' short-term program with a view to introducing participants to the more mainstream and established clubs and venues. The interviewee feels that whereas young unemployed people are not specifically catered for, their ability to access the leisure services is not particularly diminished because of this. He gives the example of standard 'off peak' concession times for several services. The young unemployed who have a degree of unobligated free time can take advantage of this type of concession as well as the general public.

Other possible ideas to increase the participation rate of the young unemployed would be to 'link up' with those agencies that predominantly deal with this group (Skillshare, the Balga Detached Youth Project). This would provide information about the leisure needs of the group as well as providing an avenue to inform them of the services available. These types of partnerships would allow appropriate concessions to be identified.

Bradford

The Bradford authority is a small locality in terms of size and population. The philosophy of leisure service delivery is one of constantly reassessing the delivery of services to the community, 'rather than a higher level of policy making, lip service type of philosophy, it is very much a hands on, get in and do it and deliver...' philosophy. The Council provides a range of leisure services and programs on a termly basis and liaises with other service providers to ensure facilities are well utilised.

This philosophy/policy is only partially consistent with the interviewees personal philosophy of leisure service delivery. He feels that a more 'strategic manner' of delivery and more 'direction' would mean a more focused delivery. Regular evaluations would allow Council to identify trends and respond more accurately to demand. The current policy does not 'cater enough for youth' and as such an analysis needs to be done in order to tailor leisure service delivery to this group. A more integrated and coordinated approach would be beneficial.

The current economic climate has not affected leisure service delivery in the Bradford region. 'At this point in time Council has been consistent with its commitment of funds towards leisure services...'. Services are not currently leased out to private contractors. Private groups operate within Shire facilities but the running of specific leisure services remains a Shire function.

There are presently no concession rates for leisure activities for the unemployed, seniors or students. If an organisation or club wished to hire a hall they would receive a 'considerable' discount. Discounts are assessed on a 'merits basis', 'Council acknowledges that some groups can't pay, and if it is in the public interest the officers have a discretion of applying that (merits case)'. For leisure courses there is an option to pay the total cost over a period of time if the participant cannot afford the full fee upfront.

The interviewee agrees that young people should be encouraged to lead healthy lifestyles. 'It's absolutely crucial because there's a lot of evidence to suggest that unemployed people and young people are not as healthy as mainstream residents and it's a crucial issue that needs to be addressed'. However, there are no specific programs aimed to increase the participation of the young unemployed in leisure activities. The current programs are structured in terms of time and cost 'so it's quite open to unemployed young people, and they are encouraged to participate'.

The interviewee considers that Council would be supportive in the future of implementing programs tailored for the young unemployed, 'I would hope that Council would be very open to ideas in terms of providing sport and recreational activities aimed at those who are unemployed'. He concedes that current resources would need to be re-organized to accommodate this.

If additional funding was made available from external sources (such as the Office of Youth Affairs, Healthway) the implementing of such programs would be more likely to go ahead. Presently, the Council would have difficulty in absorbing the extra costs of transport to and from facilities, as well as other practical considerations, 'funding would be a problem'.

No formal measures are undertaken to identify young unemployed people in the Shire. The Bradford Shire receives 'direct referrals' of unemployed young people from other organisations as well as conducting programs for the Ministry of Justice, but it is 'difficult to specifically target young people in terms of individuality'.

A 'balance' of both specific and mainstream programs would be preferred, 'singling out those who are unemployed (by using target programs) is not necessarily beneficial'. The identified benefit of participation in mainstream programs is their interactions with the general community. A preference is to provide monetary concessions and promote mainstream activities 'to get them involved'. There is an understanding that 'youth is a very important stage in peoples' development' and they may need extra support. Specific programs may be of benefit to this extent. Such activities would be a 'stepping stone' to mainstream activities.

Any implemented activities would take into account the amount of unobligated free time the young unemployed have. If a particular trend was identified any program would take this into account '... otherwise the program would not work. It would have to be at the times that they think most suitable'.

Ideas for increasing participation include 'looking at the types of programs that we are offering and perhaps make them more suitable and more appealing...' (he concedes that current programs across the board tend to target an older age group). Activities such as team sports are identified, if young unemployed people 'come to Council with ideas we can give them support to help run with it - not necessarily monetary support but information and access to resources'.

Melton

The Melton Council believes that it provides leisure services and facilities as a community service. The philosophy is one of a partnership between Council and community clubs and organisations. Access and equality are paramount, 'we strongly try and accommodate everybody into anything that we are either building, running or programming'.

This philosophy/policy is consistent with the interviewee's personal philosophy a 'majority' of the time. 'I have a problem from a human service point of view, I don't think everything needs a dollar value.' It is not feasible to put a dollar value on such areas as 'healthy people in your community' and 'happy people'. There is a frustrating element when a leisure need is identified but it cannot be addressed due to the 'monetary value' of providing the service. The interviewee considers some services should be provided if the community value element is such that it overrides the cost of providing the service.

He concedes that 'economic rationalism' has had an affect. Council is very 'budget orientated' and this can have an effect on the 'quality' of the service provided. Allowances are made for the economic situation of the community. For example, grants will be made to clubs to help them 'start up'. Fees may be waived on a 'merits basis' for some activities if a community benefit can be identified for doing so.

At present, the Melton Council does not lease out services to private contractors. Council will contract out for special projects, such as feasibility studies, but all leisure services (recreation centres and aquatic centres) are controlled by the Shire.

Concessions are made for disadvantaged sections of the community. Pensioners receive a discount for general access to venues. There are off-peak rates for the general community. There are concession rates for the unemployed. The Shire also encourages sporting clubs to take into account that not all sections of the community can afford full-fees. The Shire encourages a 'sliding scale' of memberships. The Melton Council is presently considering '... trying to incorporate some sort of pay-back system where clubs are reimbursed (by the Shire) for actually doing that (sliding scale)'.

The interviewee agrees 'absolutely' that young unemployed people should be encouraged to lead healthy lifestyles. To this end the series of off-peak concession times at various venues is geared to encourage the young unemployed to participate in activities. The council will 'actively work with groups to put in place schemes that do those sorts of things'. At present there is no specific program tailored for the young unemployed. He considers that Council may be prepared to implement such programs if 'it had tangible outcomes and if it was dollar friendly'. It is probable that such programs would only run if external funding in the form of grants could be obtained. Partnerships with existing community organisations would be preferable.

The interviewee identifies Melton as having the 'highest youth unemployment rates in the State and so it is a very, very big target for Council'. There are two main methods of identifying of the young unemployed. The Council uses the Australian Bureau of Statistics data as well as information collected by the Community Development Officer. The CDO liaises with Social Security in order to 'get those numbers direct from them'. No formal research has been undertaken in the region.

A combination of both specific and mainstream programs is considered the most appropriate way of encouraging participation. The benefits the young unemployed would derive from a specific recreation/leisure program would be the defining factor as to whether or not such activities would run again 'targeting a specific group for a specific purpose (is) as appropriate as mainstreaming, depending on the issues you are trying to address'.

Any such programs would take into account the amount of unobligated free time the young unemployed have. There is the option to '... offer more of a variety really of different things that they could do with their leisure time rather than say someone who is working 9 to 5'. There is the understanding that 'their leisure needs are completely different'. Any activities would be targeted with this in mind. A win-win situation would be one of maximising the usage of a facility which is effectively empty during off-peak times by allowing free entrance to the young unemployed. Whereas no profit is generated, the facility is still being used for its basic purpose.

Other ideas to encourage participation include 'simply getting the information out there'. Advertising on television as well as in the local papers to generate 'word-of-mouth' about events. Liaising with other organisations that are 'regularly in touch' with the group is one other possibility. Once it has been established that there is a need in a certain area, activities can be introduced targeting those areas frequented by the young unemployed. There would be communication with 'key peer leaders' in order to disseminate information as well as gain information about leisure requirements. A 'voucher system' is also proposed for the Melton region. Sporting equipment would be available in the same manner as library books, this would take the burden off the cost of equipment of the young person and encourage them to take up a sport.

Cranston

The policy of Cranston is to provide opportunities for the community to access all forms of recreation from community and local government sources. A focus on service and acceptable financial returns is of prime importance. The philosophy is one of providing stimulating recreation experiences, to encourage health, wellness, safety and enjoyment, in a cost-effective manner.

The philosophy and policy of Cranston Council is consistent with the interviewee's personal philosophy. Recreation is seen as a 'total unit', 'it doesn't matter if you sweat or if you paint it is all recreation'. Promotion of a healthy lifestyle includes a mental element as well as physical; 'we promote wellness as an ideal'. 'Basically what we (Shire) are doing fits in with my personal views'.

Changes in the economic climate have had an impact upon service delivery and community participation. The 'economic philosophy' is causing changes; 'we are looking at running smarter, more efficiently...' The Shire is reassessing how much to charge for services, whether it is feasible to lease aspects out. The Shire is aware that participation rates go 'up and down' based on disposable income. Some services may generate a greater financial return if contracted out.

Some elements of the leisure and recreation services are leased out to private contractors. The City operates and staffs its major recreation and aquatic centres, but contracts out the operation of its golf course. The arrangements are on a commission basis. The contractor receives a commission on bookings and operates a shop and kiosk for which he pays the Shire rent. The benefits of this arrangement include the public having access to a professionally run facility (the contractor is a golf professional) which the Shire may not have the skills base to operate. The contractor has the course maintained by the Shire up to a standard that attracts patronage. The objectives of the contractor are consistent with those of the Shire, 'we make them so'. Leases will not be given to contractors who will not adhere to the philosophy of service delivery that the Shire prescribes.

Concessions are made to encourage the participation of disadvantaged segments of the community. There is a 'pensioner rate' and a 'Seniors Card rate' which allow discounted participation during the week but not on weekends. There is a recognition that sections of the community may not have the type of income which allows participation in some activities, '... that's why we structure programs accordingly and get subsidies from Healthways ... so those sorts of people (can participate)' even though they have limited finances. There is no concession rate for unemployed people, there are however a range of concessions 'which apply to a whole range of people but which would definitely help out unemployed people as well'.

The interviewee agrees that young unemployed people should be encouraged to lead a healthy lifestyle, 'just as much as anybody in the community should be encouraged to lead a healthy lifestyle'. The Shire of Cranston does not presently conduct programs aimed specifically at this group. He considers that the Shire provides several opportunities for the young unemployed to participate in a healthy lifestyle. He gives as an example the access the community has to the river system. "You can canoe on it, sail on it, cycle around it, swim...". A recreation program that targets youth participation is currently running; a percentage of those participants are young unemployed. The Shire will also support programs proposed by community groups by providing facilities at a reduced rate.

The interviewee considers that the Shire of Cranston would be prepared to implement a program targeting the young unemployed. Proposed schemes would be assessed on a merits basis. Any proposal would be generated from the community. The Shire would give practical support in the form of provision of facilities. There is also the possibility that the Council would 'pick up the tab' if such a program filled certain criteria which allowed the activity to be paid for from a specific 'recreation budget'.

At present there is no formal process to identify the young unemployed in the Shire. The Council employs two youth workers who 'make a conscious effort to contact them (young unemployed) through their programs'.

The interviewee would be in favour of a combination of both specific and mainstream programs. 'I think you would use special programs to get hold of them...' with a view to encouraging mainstream participation. The amount of unobligated free time the young unemployed have would be taken into account when programming activities for them - 'my suggestion would be ... look when these kids are available, afternoons and evenings it's the whole community, ... but if you wanted to target young unemployed people, why not target them during the day.'

Other ideas to increase participation include employing someone to act as a 'catalyst'. By employing staff whose job it is to generate programs and activities the Shire could more effectively provide those services that would be most utilised by the group. Community ties could also be developed and resources more effectively used.

Brinkley

The Brinkley Shire Council is the major provider of leisure services in the region. Its philosophy of service delivery recognizes leisure as being an important factor in enhancing the quality of life for residents of the City. The Shire seeks to foster equality of access to leisure and recreation services for the community.

This philosophy in general is consistent with the interviewee's personal philosophy. He would like to see Council involved more in the 'actual delivery of programs' rather than simply the provision of facilities. 'I think there's a lot of areas of the population of the City not accessing (the) different programs that are available...'. He feels that a greater provision of resources and staffing is needed in order to address this issue. There is also greater scope for more 'forward planning' and for the Council to be better organized and more pro-active in setting up programs. The community would then be in a better position to know the types of facilities they can expect '2,3,4,5 years down the track'.

He considers that local government is 'going through a fairly significant period of change (due to) the national competition policy...' There is a strong 'push' for them to look very closely at the services they provide in order to justify why the private sector should not be providing some leisure services to the community. If it is considered that private contractors could deliver the service more economically and efficiently then the strategy is for Council to divest itself of these areas.

Many leisure services are leased out to private contractors; an example is the 'main recreation centre' which has been leased for over 12 years. The interviewee sees 'some pluses and minuses' with leasing arrangements. Whereas the Council is no longer responsible for operating deficits in this area, and this is to Council's financial advantage, there is a 'fairly strong community perception' that service delivery levels have 'fallen away'. The drop in service delivery effectiveness is due to the 'financial agenda' of the contractors, maximising profit may require cutting corners in service delivery, 'the danger is you compromise your service levels...'. Programs that the Shire would be prepared to run may not be acceptable to contractors due to less chance of generating profit.

The Council has definite expectations in terms of the quality of service delivery and range of programs. The interviewee concedes that the objectives of the contractors (profit maximisation) can cause 'conflict there, without question' with the objectives and philosophy of Council. There is a danger that 'you lose control of the type of service that you want to provide for the community and to some extent the quality aspect'. The diversity of recreation options potentially suffers if services are leased to private contractors. 'Theoretically' the contractors objectives are consistent with those of the Council, but the 'reality is that at the end of the day that the financial agenda overrides some of the other factors'. Once a service has been leased out 'we have limited control'.

Concessions are made for participation of disadvantaged segments of the community. Seniors receive a 50 percent concession to the aquatic centre, and a range of different charges exist for people on 'various pensions'. Various community groups receive discounts on the hiring of venues. There are no concessions specifically for the unemployed.

The young unemployed should 'most definitely' be encouraged to lead a healthy lifestyle. Whereas there are specific events tailored to the youth of the region there are no programs in place aimed specifically at the young unemployed. The interviewee considered that Council 'would be very keen' to implement programs specifically for the young unemployed, 'at the end of the day it comes back to the allocation of resources and dollars'. There is currently no formal process for identifying the young unemployed in the Brinkley region.

The interviewee confesses to being 'in two minds' about the advantages of specific and mainstream programs. 'Ideally they would participate in mainstream programs...'. The use of specific programs would be an advantage in addressing the 'lack of self esteem' and 'lack of confidence to take that step (into mainstream programs)' it is perceived the young unemployed suffer from. Specific programs would allow a degree of skill development and empowerment to become involved in mainstream activities. There is 'room' for both types of programs in the delivery of leisure and recreation services to the young unemployed.

The amount of unobligated free time this group has would be taken into account when programming activities, 'I think that's important and it is something we need to give more emphasis to'. He suggested that the current off-peak concession times were aimed at addressing this concern in general, but 'It's not something that is focused on providing opportunities for young unemployed people'.

His other ideas for encouraging participation in leisure and recreation programs include 'working more closely' with people in the youth field. This would enable the Shire to identify who the young unemployed are and 'make them aware of the range of options available'. There would also be the opportunity to 'talk to them about what programs and services they would like to see developed in our area, finding out what their needs are'. A better utilisation of existing 'scarce resources' would be achieved. Local government needs to 'shift with the times' and understand the leisure trends of this group, there needs to be recognition that the more traditional activities such as football and other team sports may not be enough.

Preston

The philosophy of the Preston Shire with regards to the provision and delivery of leisure services is one of planning, facilitating and delivering a cost effective and comprehensive recreation service that is affordable and accessible. Community based participation is encouraged in a wide range of activities with a view to providing a service that allows for the widest participation by the community as possible.

'Generally' philosophy is consistent with the interviewee's personal views on service delivery. However, 'how that philosophy is put into practice is sometimes a different matter'. 'I suppose we (Council) look at recreation with some blinkered vision ... I think the demand by the community for a quality of life warrants greater attention both on a funding and resource level'.

The changes in the economic climate have had 'a direct effect on capital works in particular'. Budgetary constraints have meant that the implementation of new programs targeting a specific area of the population now requires some level of subsidy before Council will implement such a program. 'Predominantly however, the major impact has been on the minimal capacity. We now have to raise State or Federal funding support towards major or even small scale infrastructure'.

Some leisure services in the Preston district are leased out to private contractors, "there is a cost effectiveness about it (leasing)'. Another advantage he identifies is that 'the level of service able to be provided is enhanced'. The objectives of the contractors 'are and are not' consistent with the objectives of the Shire. Where individual groups have leased out a multi-purpose facility (he gives the example of a basketball association leasing out an entire recreation centre) the objectives 'aren't always the same'. The contractors' objective is primarily to develop 'their sport', due to the nature of the centre being a multi-purpose facility the Shire would 'like their objective to be primarily aimed at increasing the range of sporting opportunities or leisure opportunities and not focusing on one particular aspect'.

Concessions are made in order to encourage the participation of disadvantaged sections of the community. A 'discount rate' or 'free access' is available to a wide range of charitable organizations. If events have a 'charitable nature' or a wide spread community benefit for a group that is disadvantaged these concessions apply. There are specific concession rates for 'unemployed youth' to access specific leisure venues.

Young unemployed people should 'definitely' be encouraged to lead healthy lifestyles. 'They obviously have leisure issues ... their need to improve their own self-image, self-worth and self-esteem'. At present there is no program in place targeting the young unemployed, 'the capacity of the organisation to provide that is limited at the present time'. However, the Council would consider such programs if this group became a 'priority focus' for the Shire. Often issues tend to be 'put on the back burner, or receive a lower priority than other projects'. At present many programs are targeted at the general youth population and it is felt that this group receives enough support. There is the opportunity for the young unemployed to access the 'informal recreation services' within the region. Examples include parks, coastline and skate board facilities.

Information regarding the identification of the young unemployed in the Shire is obtained via 'external agencies' such as Family and Children's Services, Social security and the Australian Bureau of Statistics. 'Community workshops' are also used to identify select groups within the community. A Youth Officer has conducted interviews with 'young people' as well as run a series of 'community forums' to discover the leisure needs of young people. The young unemployed have been identified as part of this process.

The interviewee is in favour of both specific and mainstream programs for the young unemployed. 'Primarily, I like to see mainstream programs more than specific, but I understand that with any target group there are specific needs associated with that group'. His personal philosophy is that programs that are introduced 'on a mainstream level' should incorporate the special needs of the target group 'you wish to be involved in that program'. Any mainstream activities should provide such concessions and opportunities for participation that specific groups will wish to take part in. 'I think that the mainstream programs perhaps diminish the opportunity for peer group pressure to be enforced'.

The amount of unobligated free time that young unemployed people have would be taken into account when programming for the group. Programs would primarily run during off-peak times when 'working people tend not to dominate the time slot'.

Other ideas to increase the participation of the young unemployed include involving 'them in the decision making process'. By consulting prior to any program development there is the opportunity to assess potential time slots, the manner in which the program will be administered, costs to participants and transport and other practical issues.

Oakwood

The philosophy of the Oakwood Council is to optimise the leisure potential of the community by providing and encouraging the use of a variety of leisure and recreation activities. The Council aims to improve the customer satisfaction level of recreation and leisure services and raise the operational efficiency of service delivery.

This philosophy is consistent with the interviewee's own personal philosophy of leisure and recreation delivery. There are on occasion difficulties in achieving a balance between aspects of the policies. Whereas there is a policy of raising 'operational efficiency' the interviewee concedes 'we are not in a commercial environment', there are social and community responsibilities. 'Business efficiency' needs to make way on occasions to the Shire's social obligations of service provision; 'often we do things we would not do in a commercial situation'.

Changes in the economic climate have had an effect on service delivery, 'if you mean ... competition in the market place it certainly has'. The Shire has had to become more competitive with private and other local government services. The services offered are marketed 'more smartly' and 'we have an eye on our competitors - if they are dropping prices then we have to respond to that'. In terms of people having 'less money going around' the impact has been minimal, services are still well utilised.

Some leisure services are leased out to private contractors; 'in the main they are not'. If a program or service requires a degree of skill and specialty that the Shire feels it does not possess, the service is tendered out in order that it is run by the best qualified people (he gave an example of the golf course which is leased to golf professionals). The objectives of the contractors are consistent with those of the Council, 'they wouldn't win a tender if they were not. Its really that simple'. He appreciates that all tenders will have profit as their motivation, the 'trick is to reflect Council objectives in the tender process'. Mechanisms are built into the lease to ensure contractors meet Council expectations regarding program and service delivery. Community service obligations are balanced against contractors profit maximising objectives.

Concessions are made in order to encourage the participation of disadvantaged sections of the community. Whereas the Council does not offer direct concessions for entry into venues or programs there are concessions 'geared towards the general community'. He gave an example of the ability to buy 'bulk tickets'; it is possible to buy a book of tickets that allows entrance to venues. By buying in bulk the individual receives a discount. There are no concessions based on categorisations such as senior citizens, unemployed, etc. He believes that services the and facilities are already heavily subsidised so providing concessions on top of this is financially not feasible.

The interviewee considers that the young unemployed should be encouraged to lead healthy lifestyles ('what are you in the business for if you say no?'). But at present there are no programs specifically tailored for the young unemployed. The Shire would be prepared to implement such programs if 'external funding' became available. Such 'financial partnerships', combined with a 'great proposal', is the only way in the present financial climate Council would be prepared to target such a specific group.

There have been no formal evaluations to identify young unemployed people in the region. Both Youth Workers and Community Development workers use 'fairly good networks and have an ear to the ground' with regard to identifying youth issues and the needs of specific groups. The Council also uses Australian Bureau of Statistics data to identify segments of the community. At present these statistics have not been used to identify the young unemployed.

The interviewee is in favour of both specific and mainstream programs. There are plans to implement specific recreation programs in the future directed at the young unemployed, '... let's offer the young unemployed programs or packages in some way that is clearly for the young unemployed'.

His ideas to increase the participation of the young unemployed include involving them more in the process 'so they can have some input at (this) level...'. There is also the possibility of using general recreation centres 'a bit smarter in terms of promoting them and marketing'. He gives an example of promoting off peak times to the community in general with a view to the young unemployed accessing the program by advertising the fact that the service exists to agencies that may have dealings with them, such as the CES. By making it known that an opportunity to participate exists it is hoped the young unemployed may access the services.

Ravenswood

Ravenswood is a rural centre and as such sport and recreation are important aspects of community life. The Ravenswood Council is very flexible in its service delivery to the community. The service consists of very few facilities and the philosophy is one of providing subsidised access to this limited range of resources. This policy is consistent with that of the interviewee. There is a great deal of leeway to run and deliver services in relation to community demand.

Changes in the economic climate have affected the strategies for service delivery; 'there is a greater emphasis on making the dollar go further'. There has been a change from a paying fees up-front to a pay-as-you-use system – 'whilst they pay more on a weekly basis they don't feel it, they don't have to budget to have $100 at the beginning of the season but they in fact pay $100 through the year'.

Aspects of leisure services are leased out. Whereas the Shire will still pay the operational costs (he gives the example is given of pool chemicals and water costs for the local pool), the management services may be leased out. He considers that it is more financially viable to lease out this aspect of the service due to the cost of award rates and the inflexibility of Shire employees. The objectives of contractors are consistent with those of the Shire.

Concessions are made to the disadvantaged sections of the community. Seniors are given free entrance to specific venues during off peak times. There are provisions to purchase 'season tickets' to venues, which reduces the cost across the season. Whereas the interviewee agrees that the young unemployed should be encouraged to lead a healthy lifestyle there are no specific programs in place at present. On previous occasions programs that have been aimed at the young unemployed have not been well utilised or profitable so they have been discontinued; '... it will be to a degree dollar driven, but you need the numbers and that's one of the problems in the country.' The Council would be prepared to implement programs aimed at the young unemployed, but would be 'reluctant' to subsidise them due to the reduced cost of entry to venues that is already in place.

No formal measures have been undertaken to identify the young unemployed in the region. He considers that if there were a need to identify it would be viable to approach the CES to try and establish the numbers.

The interviewee is not in favour of specific programs developed for the young unemployed due to being 'reluctant to sort of label them'. This is an important consideration in a small country because of to the nature of the community. It is preferable to promote mainstream programs 'open to everybody' and provide the opportunities for participation. Previous activities have been affected by the groups' 'motivation' to be involved. He considers the group prefers unstructured activities on Shire facilities such as football ovals and basketball courts.

His other ideas to involve the young unemployed include conducting research to establish the types of activities which would be appropriate. It is important not to make assumptions concerning which programs should be conducted and at what times. It is also important in the country context to take into account the 'seasonal aspect' of work given the impact such work has on the utilisation of facilities. Practical considerations are particularly important; he gives an example of the difficulties of transport for a widely dispersed population.

Selected Public Provider Variables

The variables in the questionnaire to public providers were: organisation policy; personal philosophy; economic demands; contracting services; equity provisions; unemployment programs; and program types. The similarities and differences are discussed below.

Organisation policy: The policies of the nine local authorities were fairly consistent in that they wished to be inclusive of the whole community in the provision of facilities and services. Providers had their own way of implementing local authority policy. In the case of Wentworth, they would do so by direct services and supporting self-help agencies and associations. Equity in planning, coordinating, and promotion of services was a valued ideal for Shenton. Melton formed partnerships with clubs and associations. Cranston provided for health and enjoyment outcomes. Brinkley's program was to enhance the quality of life and Oakwood planned for a variety of activities. Only one authority, namely, Preston linked its objectives with financial viability, by providing cost-effective services. Ravenswood had no written policy, but was flexible enough to encourage change. Individual responses to organisational policy are listed in Table 8.1.

Table 8.1
Organisation Policy

Local Authority	Organisation Policy
Wentworth	Provision of leisure opportunities to all sectors of the community by direct & supportive self-help services.
Shenton	To plan, manage, co-ordinate & promote services, facilities & resources on basis of equity.
Bradford	Constant communication with the community to satisfy perceived community needs.
Melton	Leisure provision viewed as a community service; philosophy of partnership between council, clubs & organisations.
Cranston	Provision of opportunities for access to all forms of recreation to stimulate & encourage health & enjoyment.
Brinkley	Recognises leisure to enhance quality of life of residents; equality of access seen as important.
Preston	Planning, facilitating of cost effective services with widest possible community access.
Oakwood	Optimise the leisure potential of the community by providing a variety of recreational activities.
Ravenswood	No written policy, but flexibility exists for service delivery.

Although philosophies of each local authority were inclusive, they had various methods of implementing policy. If these fragmented approaches were integrated they would form a basis for a coordinated policy for local authorities in the Perth metropolitan area.

Personal philosophy: The personal philosophies of the nine recreation officers were generally consistent with the policies set out by their local authorities. However, each one made a qualifying statement. At Wentworth, the recreation officer said he was responsible for driving policy. The focus of Shenton was on localisation of facilities and services to encourage accessibility. At Bradford, the policy did little for youth and needed coordination and integration. It was hard to put a dollar value on all recreation services in Melton. Brinkley would like direct delivery of services, rather than the mere provision of facilities. There was disappointment in Preston as policies weren't being implemented. Oakwood experienced conflicts between service delivery and business efficiency. In Ravenswood, service delivery was totally consistent with local authority policy. Table 8.2 indicates the personal philosophies of the recreation officers responsible for the delivery of services.

Table 8.2
Personal Policy

Local Authority	Personal Policy
Wentworth	Agency policy consistent with the interviewee's position; responsible for driving leisure service delivery and defining performance
Shenton	Consistent with that of employer; leisure seen as best provided at local level, accessible in places where people live & work.
Bradford	Current policy does not cater of the younger population as much as it should; more integrated & co-ordinated approach required.
Melton	Consistent with council policy; not always possible to put a dollar value on a human service.
Cranston	Consistent with that of council, while adding mental to physical health.
Brinkley	Consistent with council policy; would like to see services rather than just facility provision.
Preston	Philosophy consistent with council policy; but stated policies not always implemented.
Oakwood	Consistent with council philosophy, but some inconsistency with service delivery & business efficiency.
Ravenswood	Service delivery policy consistent with those of local authority.

There were inconsistencies between the organisation policies and personal philosophies of recreation officers. The emphasis of services and manner in which they were delivered varied in each case. Thus organisation and philosophies did not have a good fit.

Economic demands: Services in seven of the nine local authorities were affected by the national competition policy. In Wentworth, Council had to be more accountable for financial losses. Services were assessed against the national competition policy in Shenton. Economic rationalisation had a big effect on services, budgets and quality of services in Melton. It also meant reassessment of services and fees and charges in Cranston. In Brinkley contracting out was a preferred option, while Preston was constrained in facility development because of budget cuts. Oakwood was required to be more competitive with public recreation outlets. The small local authority of Bradford and Ravenswood, a rural shire on the City fringe did not report the national competition policy affecting services. The various ways in which local authorities responded to economic concerns are listed in Table 8.3.

The national competition policy influenced how services should be delivered. Concerns about being competitive in the leisure services market consumed local authorities and inclusion of deserving people may have been overlooked.

Contracting services: The local authorities of Shenton, Cranston, Brinkley, Preston and Oakwood had some services leased out to private contractors. Wentworth was in the process of contracting out services. Bradford, Melton and Ravenswood had facilities and services controlled by the Council. In each case where services were contracted out, the objectives of the contractors had to comply with those of the council. If the objectives of contractors were not consistent with those of Council, a contract would not be awarded. However, there were instances at Oakwood and Brinkley, where financial objectives conflicted with social ones. Attitudes towards contracting out are listed in Table 8.4.

Table 8.3
Economic Demands

Local Authority	Economic Demands
Wentworth	Services affected by current economic climate; Council accountable for financial losses resulting from 'national competition' policy.
Shenton	Services affected by economic climate; services assessed against the background of national competition policy.
Bradford	Current economic climate has little impact on service delivery; council provides funds for service delivery.
Melton	Economic rationalism having an influence on budgets & quality of services offered, but assistance still offered 'start up' new clubs.
Cranston	Economic climate requires reassessment of service delivery in relation to charges & use of leisure contractors.
Brinkley	National competition policy taking effect in council's decisions; contracting of services preferred if financially advantageous.
Preston	Affected service delivery; constraints on capital works & budgets requires subsidies from external sources.
Oakwood	Big effect as the council has shifted strategy to more competitive modes of service delivery.
Ravenswood	More emphasis on 'making the dollar go further'; pay as you use system introduced to counter difficulties in paying upfront fees

The data revealed that contracting out was embraced by the majority of local authorities. This was done for purposes of efficiency. However, although some local authorities made contractors comply with council objectives, it was felt that financial objectives conflicted with social ones.

Equity provisions: All of the nine local authorities had some sort of equity provisions at least for certain sections of the community. Seniors came out best in Wentworth, Melton, Cranston, Brinkley, Preston and Ravenswood. In Wentworth,

Table 8.4
Contracting Out

Local Authority	Contracting Services
Wentworth	Plans underway to lease out services to private contractors, but contractors' economic interests must be balanced with community interests.
Shenton	Outsourced services should benefit contactor & council; only those with mutual benefits are leased out.
Bradford	No services or facilities are leased out; services directly delivered.
Melton	No leases to private clubs.
Cranston	Some aspects contracted out on a commission basis; objectives of contractors must be consistent with those of the council.
Brinkley	Many services leased out to private contractors; financial objectives often in conflict with social objectives.
Preston	Some services contracted out; objectives of contractors & council not always congruent; biases towards certain sports.
Oakwood	Some services contracted out, especially those where greater efficiency is recognised by a private operator.
Ravenswood	Facilities maintained by council, but services may be leased out.

juniors were not charged fees. Except for Melton and Preston, young unemployed people were not given concessions. At Bradford no concessions were awarded to individuals, but groups were treated on a merit basis. The status of services on an equity basis is listed in Table 8.5.

Equity provisions were in place for seniors and in some cases for juniors. Just two local authorities took into account the interests of the unemployed. This indicates that this class of people are either not taken into account or authorities find it difficult to identify and process them for services.

Unemployment programs: All the local authority re-creation officers supported the promotion of healthy lifestyles

Table 8.5
Equity Provisions

Local Authority	Equity Provisions
Wentworth	Concessions for services exist for senior citizens, juniors & individuals using specific services; no concessions for young unemployed.
Shenton	Concessions & subsidies for events are available to the community; young unemployed not targeted specifically.
Bradford	No concessions to any sectors of the community, but hire of facilities by interest groups are considerably discounted.
Melton	Concessions available to disadvantaged, including unemployeds; off-peak rates available to the general community; sliding scale rates available.
Cranston	Concessions & discounts available to some community segments, but none exist for unemployed people.
Brinkley	Concessions made for certain segments, such as seniors, but no specific steps taken for the unemployed
Preston	Range of concessions offered – discounts & free access; concessions extended to young unemployed.
Oakwood	No direct concessions as services are heavily subsidised; bulk tickets provide further discounts.
Ravenswood	Reductions for seniors, 'season tickets' are available, but nothing for young unemployed.

for young people. However, none conducted specific programs for the unemployed. Melton encouraged participation at its facilities during off-peak periods. Cranston encouraged no cost activities by promoting the use of parks and the river. The authorities of Brinkley, Wentworth, Shenton, Bradford and Oakwood would conduct programs for the unemployed if external funds were available. Shenton would do it in partnership with private agencies. Responses for programs for the unemployed are in Table 8.6.

Specific programs for the unemployed were non-existent. However, there was a willingness to conduct programs or include the jobless if appropriate funding was available.

Table 8.6
Unemployment Programs

Local Authority	Unemployment Programs
Wentworth	Favours mainstream & specific programs; cost is a factor; if external funding is available, there is no problem running programs; no steps taken to identify the unemployed.
Shenton	No specific programs for the unemployed, but they can be set up with partnership with other or private agencies.
Bradford	No specific programs exist, but existing costs are not prohibitive. Council would support specific programs if funding is available.
Melton	Healthy lifestyle encouraged; off-peak participation designed to promote participation.
Cranston	Although healthy lifestyles are encouraged, there are no specific programs for the unemployed; use of river facilities & parks are supported.
Brinkley	Healthy lifestyle programs exist for youth, but not specifically for the unemployed; with funds available, council would implement.
Preston	Healthy lifestyles should be encouraged, but council do not have the means & the group is not a focus for them.
Oakwood	No programs exist for unemployed people, but council would consider if funds were available.
Ravenswood	Young unemployed people should be encouraged to lead healthy lifestyles, but no programs exist.

Program types: The preferences for program types are listed in Table 8.7. Most local authorities favoured mainstream programs for the unemployed. Shenton, Bradford, Melton, Cranston, Brinkley and Oakwood expressed a mix of mainstream and specific programs. Specific programs were meant to be stepping stones for integration into mainstream programs. The Officer for Brinkley suggested specific programs for skill development and empowerment. The Bradford representative saw specific programs as an integration into mainstream ones.

Table 8.7
Program Types

Local Authority	Program Types
Wentworth	Young jobless need access to facilities & services; finance & time availability should be assessed.
Shenton	Support for mainstream in preference to specific programs; use of passive space for those who do not wish structured leisure services.
Bradford	A balance between specific & mainstream programs; mainstream programs are more integrative & specific ones seen as a 'stepping stone'.
Melton	Combination of mainstream & specific programs preferred.
Cranston	Support for both specific & mainstream programs, with the former seen as the first step to the latter.
Brinkley	Supports integration into mainstream, but sees some advantages in specific programs eg. Skill development, empowerment.
Preston	In favour of mainstream programs which incorporate concessions.
Oakwood	Specific & mainstream programs favoured.
Ravenswood	Specific programs seen as unsuitable; lack of numbers and motivation seen as problems.

There was overwhelming preference for mainstream programs with specific programs being run as stepping stones into mainstream leisure. However, mainstream leisure was seen not for skill development at purpose built facilities, but also in the natural environment.

This completes the examination of the seven variables affecting leisure participation. The philosophies and policies of local councils were important in that they were all inclusive. So were those who integrated equity issues into participation policy. However, equity considerations applied invariably to seniors, but not to the young unemployed.

9

Findings, Recommendations and Conclusions

The purpose of this study was to determine the impact of unemployment on young adults and to ameliorate its effects through sport and recreation programs, so as to induce participation and promote commitment to healthy lifestyles. To achieve this purpose there questions were raised: (1) What is the impact of unemployment on young adults? (2) How can sport and recreation ameliorate the impact of job loss? (3) How can public sport and recreation programs be delivered to young unemployed adults to promote commitment and healthy lifestyles?

In order to answer these questions, the study was planned in two stages, an exploratory and confirmatory stage. The first phase was interactive and cross-sectional. It consisted of workshops with young unemployed males and females between the ages of 18 and 30. The second phase, was also interactive and involved lifestyle and depth interviews with young people. Depth interviews were also conducted with providers of leisure and recreation services in order to find out the problems involved in offering programs to the unemployed. Participant and provider perspectives to the problems were addressed. These views are now stated alongside each of the questions together with the findings.

Findings

Question 1: What is the impact of unemployment on young adults?

Unemployment causes several types of impact. These could be on self, family, job search, reduced income and leisure. Since the impact on leisure is the focus of the second and third questions, effects on unemployment on leisure will be treated later. With the workshops, lifestyle and depth interviews, the impacts on unemployment were felt in the various domains of life.

Responses from the workshops revealed that unemployment impacted adversely on self. It was an unwanted and unpleasant experience characterised by shock, anger and frustration. Many saw themselves as victims. The outcomes of job loss caused boredom, depression and low levels of motivation. It was no surprise then, that large proportions of responses reflected low self-esteem and confidence.

With the lifestyle interviews responses on the impact of unemployment on the self were evenly divided between being depressed, angry and bitter on the one hand and being positive and relieved on the other. Reasons that caused depression and anger were the lack of personal direction, misplaced loyalty to an employer, hassles at work and conditions' beyond one's control. The positive outlook was the opportunity to study further, travel, not having to deal with a difficult boss and the hope of reemployment.

Data from the depth interviews indicated some differences and similarities in impact between males and females. More women than men tended to be depressed and demoralised as a result of losing their job. More men felt angry, upset and anxious and financially insecure than women. Men who were optimistic about future employment soon after job loss became desperate as the length of unemployment increased. Both sexes missed the structure of work and felt positive over time after initial trauma experienced with job loss.

Responses from the workshops indicated that family perceptions compounded feelings of depression. Participants were seen as misfits, expected to look for work, expected to do more jobs in the home and were compared to siblings who may be models to imitate if in employment and not to like if unemployed. The consistency feelings of aversion, both real and imagined, fuelled arguments over trivial matters and the guilt of doing an enjoyable activity. The lifestyle interviews revealed similar findings, as many good relationships changed to poor. Some were left with little option but to physically withdraw from others in the home.

The depth interviews showed gender differences in family relationships and responsibilities. All men interviewed said that their families were supportive, but only half as many females reported such relationships. These relationships were mainly with parents. Relationships were generally positive, but there were reports of parents' anxiety and strains as the unemployment experience lengthened with both sexes. Some females said that they were seen not to be trying for work. A small number took household roles.

Unemployment meant having to search for a job. It was painful and frustrating. The majority found that skills acquired at the Job Club were very useful. They used various methods of job search. The major problems in acquiring jobs were the lack of qualifications and experience. Persistent rejections and at times the lack of acknowledgement of applications caused frustrations. Other constraints that affected job search were the lack of transport and inadequate interview clothing.

The lack of income impacted badly as it caused jobless young people to restrict a number of their customary activities. Several had to buy cheaper food. Others could not buy new clothes or had to by second-hand apparel. Socialising and entertainment were also curtailed and difficulties in paying bills increased. Some males found that surviving on their own difficult and had to move back to the family home, and females reported being confined to activities at home because of the lack of income.

Based on the above statement may be made to reflect findings on the impacts of unemployment on self, family, job search and reduced income.

Finding 1: Unemployment impacted adversely on self. It was an unwanted and unpleasant experience characterised by shock, anger and frustration. Many saw themselves as victims. They became bored, depressed and unmotivated, resulting in reduced self-esteem and confidence.

Finding 2: Family relationships often changed from good to poor. Young unemployed people were often seen as misfits, expected to look for work, expected to do more jobs in the home, and were compared unfavourably to siblings in employment. Parents' anxiety and strains were evident and arguments over trivial matters were common.

Finding 3: The job search process was painful and frustrating. Lack of qualifications and experience made reemployment remote. Despite multi-modal ways of seeking employment, job rejections and the lack of acknowledgement of applications made job search seem a waste of time.

Finding 4: Reduced income causes severe restraints in expenditure. Cheaper foods were purchased; new clothes were unaffordable; socialising and entertainment were curtailed; and withdrawal for long periods in the home was common.

Question 2: How can sport and recreation ameliorate the impact of job loss?

From the workshop responses on employment, it was clear that the vast majority of young people (89%) saw themselves as energetic, busy, happy and laidback. Self perceptions of some were as artistic and sporting persons. Employment made them feel good because they were able to set goals and have a purpose in life. It induced healthy social networks and family support. Participants were involved in a wide array of activities before unemployment. Besides television viewing, which was almost universal, team sports, individual activities, social activities and music arts and reading were mentioned in large numbers. Leisure activities accounted for 423 responses resulting in an average of 6.8 activities per person, consistent with a standard for Australian young people. Job loss had a distinct impact on leisure behaviour. Material and psychological deprivations of unemployment caused increased television viewing, less participation in active sports, more low cost and home-based activities, more time in bed and longer time taken doing tasks. Increases and decreases were reported by some in smoking and drinking – increases to alleviate frustrations and decreases because of the lack of money. For some, job loss meant more time with friends.

The lifestyle interviews revealed that for the majority of young people the quantity of home-based leisure after unemployment was the same or had increased. For a small proportion, which included those who were psychologically adversely affected, the quantity of leisure activities was reduced. Many young people were active in the home and kept busy in order to fill the large blocks of unobligated time which unemployment imposes. The leisure of those severely affected by job loss was reduced to passivity as a consequence of a lack of motivation and apparent boredom.

Organised sport was very much in the repertoire of young people's leisure for fitness before unemployment. The major reason for continuing with fitness activities was because more time was available to pursue fitness activities, some were able to release their anger and frustration, and a few found the cost of participation low enough for them to continue. The other half who had ceased participation not only diminished the quantity of fitness activities, but by disengaging reduced the quality of their leisure experience. The major reason for discontinuation of many fitness activities was a consequence of lack of money, which was felt by both males and females.

The social involvement of young people was adversely affected by job loss quantitatively and qualitatively. Lack of money was again cited for reduced social engagement with friends at venues such as pubs. Qualitatively, it was found that social networks were restricted to other unemployed friends who were in the same boat and who had mutual understanding of the deprivations of job loss. In some cases, social discomfort in the company of others led to self-imposed isolation.

Entertainment was seriously affected quantitatively by the lack of money. Without certain forms of entertainment, it could be inferred that the quality of the social and leisure world of the individual was diminished. However, getting involved in cheaper forms of entertainment and doing less with less showed favourable signs of adaptation by young people. Continuation of membership in clubs and associations was seriously affected by job loss. Unemployment caused large numbers to cease membership because of the lack of finance. Material deprivation not only caused a diminution of leisure quantitatively, but also affected the individual's overall leisure qualitatively. Those severely affected by unemployment chose to isolate themselves, but that isolation was also complemented by lack of money to continue membership.

The depth interviews showed that the use of electronics was common among both females and males. The computer, telephone, radio and hi-fi were used to fill time and for females to keep in touch with their friends especially through the use of the phone. Females tended to get involved in household chores more than males, but more males than females worked in the garden. Some watched more television and others less. Females tended to read more than males and some said that they now met their friends at home. Females were more involved in household chores of cleaning and cooking and males doing things with their hands, which required repairing and fixing skills. One male decided to give up his hobby of photography because of the lack of money.

A large proportion of young people participated in cheaper forms of recreation. These included activities such as walking, jogging, cycling and visits to parks. Six females curtailed sporting activities because of membership and transport costs. Only two males reported being involved in organised sport before job loss and they continued these activities. Males and females went out less and expressed concerns of social discomfort in the company of others. A cheaper party as often took the place of commercial recreation. The data from the workshops, lifestyle and depth interviews reveal that the quantity and quality of leisure is affected by unemployment and may be summed up as follows.

Finding 5: Except for home-based activities, unemployment tends to reduce the quantity of leisure activities out of the home. Material and psychological deprivation jointly impact on the individual to reduce the quality of the many leisure activities that young people engage in, including those in the home.

Question 3: How can public sport and recreation programs be delivered to young unemployed adults to promote commitment to healthy lifestyles.

This question was addressed during interviews with providers of leisure and sport services. Eight variables were examined. They included: organization philosophy; personal philosophy;

economic demands; contracting services; equity provisions; unemployment programs; and program types.

The policies of the nine local authorities were fairly consistent in that they intended to be inclusive of the whole community in the provision of facilities and services. The personal philosophies of the nine recreation officers were generally consistent with the policies set out by their local authorities. However, some expressed misgivings about the discrepancy between policy intent and implementation, but there were no major disagreements between organisational and personal viewpoints. Seven of the nine local authority interviewees felt the pressures of the national competition policy. They had to be accountable, programs were assessed against that policy, and budgets and quality of programs were scrutinised. The national competition policy forced several leisure providers to contract services out and if some had not already done so, they were in the process of so doing. Problems of social and financial objectives of contractors and council were being examined for congruency between both parties. There were assurances from providers that contractors would have to fall in line with council objectives if they were to secure the contract.

All nine local authorities had some forms of equity provisions. Seniors did very well, but there were no special deals for the unemployed. Concessions offered such as off-peak rates, applied to all members of the community. No local authority had any specific programs for the unemployed. However, they saw the need to support healthy lifestyles for them. Being faced with critical problems of funding and service variability, they were unable to go it alone with programs for the unemployed. All expressed willingness to run special programs if funding was available from bodies who have as their core interest the wellbeing of young unemployed people. These projects could be specifically for the unemployed, but used as a means to enter mainstream programs. There was a general consensus that young people should be included in mainstream activities. The consideration of the eight variables discussed with providers of services leads to further findings.

Finding 6: The philosophies and policies of local authorities were inclusive in that they provided for the whole community. These policies were congruent with those of the recreation officers who were responsible for sport and leisure service programs.

Finding 7: Pressures arising from the national competition policy placed sport and leisure providers under strains to make facilities financially viable, to be more accountable and to compete for the discretionary leisure dollar.

Finding 8: The economic demands placed on providers have forced them to consider other ways of delivering services especially by leasing and contracting.

Finding 9: Providers were cognisant of social objectives being sacrificed at the expense of financial objectives and were taking steps to ensure contractors aligned themselves with Council objectives.

Finding 10: Equity provision for young unemployed people was found to be wanting. No deliberate steps were taken to identify young unemployed people and to enable them to use local facilities for sport and recreation.

Finding 11: Inclusion into mainstream programs was generally supported. If specific programs were conducted, they would have to be as stepping stones for entry into mainstream programs.

Finding 12: Partnerships with external funding agencies and local authorities were welcomed, with the latter showing willingness to run specific programs.

Recommendations arising from the findings to the three questions will be developed in the following section.

Recommendations

Data from the workshops, lifestyle and depth interviews revealed that unemployment causes boredom, depression and low levels of motivation. Studies have shown that keeping occupied (Hepworth, 1980) and active (Swinburne, 1981) have a moderating effect on the negative effects of unemployment. Being occupied and active are coping strategies that are suggested.

Recommendation 1: Keeping active and occupied in meaningful activities are effective ways of counteracting the boredom and depression that job loss might cause.

It has been shown that engagement in activities that include the categories of the employment experience is associated with enhanced wellbeing (Haworth and Ducker, 1991). It is therefore important that activities engaged in include those categories.

Recommendation 2: Coping activities to enhance wellbeing may include a time structure, social contacts, a collective purpose, a feeling of identity, and regular activity. Participation in active team and individual sports provide for these areas of experience.

The job search experience was described as painful and frustrating. Study participants spent many hours at the job club, using several methods of seeking employment. They spent significant amounts of energy and time seeking a job. Those doing courses to improve their skills were also mentally challenged. If these young people consider their time was spent in a positive manner, then they should have no guilt about participating in sport or leisure activity to reward their efforts in seeking work.

Recommendation 3: After spending time and energy in the job search process, young people should feel entitled to reward themselves with active and constructive recreation activities, especially those which they were accustomed to before losing their job.

Some families perceive of unemployed young people as misfits, not trying to secure employment, expected to do more home jobs and compared unfavourably to successful siblings, and this causes disappointment to many young people. However, it is possible to turn things around in the home if young people volunteer to help, give daily or frequent accounts of attempts to seek work, are seen to be active and not sullen and make efforts to involve themselves in regular healthy activity.

Recommendation 4: Life in the home can be made more tolerable if young unemployed females and males volunteer their services to do household chores, are seen to be trying to secure work, give regular accounts of job search, are cheerful and are involved in active healthy recreation.

It was noted from the workshops that young people felt well and engaged in a range of leisure and sport activities before unemployment. This indicates that leisure and sport are important to an individual's health and wellbeing. The material and psychological deprivation caused by unemployment diminished the quality and quantity of leisure participation out of home. In the home the quantity may have increased, but the increase in quality was questionable. How then could sport and recreation ameliorate the impact of job loss? A few participants were able to preserve their health and wellbeing by engaging in low cost activities. In so doing, they prompt a crucial recommendation to ameliorate the deprivations of job loss:

Recommendation 5: Maintain a healthy and active lifestyle by substituting pre-job loss activities with low or no cost activities that deliver similar health and wellbeing activities.

The philosophies and policies of providers of sport and leisure services were inclusive. However, little was done for young people who were unemployed, despite the fact that the interviewees felt that this group needs to be encouraged to lead healthy lifestyles. It seems important therefore, that young unemployed people be identified and encouraged to participate in health inducing activity:

Recommendation 6: Providers of leisure services should make every attempt to identify and encourage young people to use local sport and recreation services through awareness campaigns.

Recommendation 7: If discounted rates are offered during off-peak times, then these should be advertised at places that young people frequent, such as job clubs and training agencies.

Given that the national competition policy is making it difficult for providers to give further discounts to already subsidised services, attempts should be made to form partnerships with unemployment agencies at which incentives may be offered to young unemployed people to use local facilities. After probing what the leisure interests of young people, case managers should be able to offer pre-paid entry cards to facilities for limited periods. When the period expires and if the individual is still unemployed, he or she might apply for a renewal for further period of time. Of course, all the checks of job search that the employment agency requires should be maintained. Where the employment agency pays for the entry, this ensures that the recreation facility manager gets the normal payment that so further payment would not be required of any user. Swipe cards used for entry are most appropriate as they do not distinguish between people that are employed and those who are not. The production of a card that identified the unemployed was seen to be stigmatising:

Recommendation 8: Working in partnership with employment and training agencies or those responsible for youth affairs, providers of sport and leisure services should arrive at agreements to supply entry cards to the unemployed for services offered at public facilities.

It was noted that equity provision served the seniors well, but does not cater for the young unemployed. If inclusive policies are in place for disadvantaged groups, then the young unemployed should not be overlooked:

Recommendation 9: Equity provision for the participation of young unemployed people in sport and leisure should not only feature in policy statements, but must be seen to be promoted and implemented.

Mainstream programs were generally supported for the unemployed. However, specific programs were supported by providers as long as they were inducements towards mainstream participation. The rationale for supporting mainstream programs was to socially integrate and assimilate the unemployed into the general community.

Recommendation 10: Mainstream programs are supported, but if specific programs are conducted for the unemployed, they should act as stepping stones towards social integration and assimilation into the general community.

The above findings and recommendations have been generated from four modes of social inquiry involving the exploratory and confirmatory stages.

Conclusions

This study sought to identify the deprivations of young unemployed males and females between the ages of 18 and 30. It also attempted to show how those deprivations could be ameliorated by enabling health inducing participation at public sport and leisure facilities. Examination of the data resulted in twelve findings, five of which impacted on self, family, job search, reduced income, leisure in the home and leisure out of the home. Seven others arose out of attempts to include unemployed young people into sport and leisure programs delivered from public facilities.

Five recommendations have been developed on personal coping strategies with the enforced bulk time that unemployment imposes, reduced income, the frustration's of job search, dealing with the family, and the effects on sport and leisure in and out of the home. Five other recommendations concern inclusive policies, equity issues to encourage health inducing participation, the promotion of activities for health benefits, partnerships with job training, employment and youth organizations and the development of programs to integrate young people into mainstream community activity. The implementation of the recommendations will ensure that serious attempts will have been made to improve the quality of like of young unemployed people in Western Australia.

APPENDICES

APPENDIX A
Youth Unemployment Workshops

Before unemployment, what kind of person were you?

Before unemployment, what sport and recreation did you participate in?

What impact did unemployment have on you?

After unemployment, what leisure activities did you participate in?

How did job loss affect relationships within the family?

How can you help yourself?

How can voluntary groups help?

How can governments help?

APPENDIX B
Youth Lifestyle Questionnaire

INTERVIEW WITH; AGE; POB; MALE/FEMALE; INTERVIEW DATE

What was your previous employment?

What is your main occupation?

What is your level of formal education?

How would you describe your present financial status?

List the towns you have lived in during your life?

When you were in employment, describe the activities that contributed to the happiness of the family?

When in employment what activities did you participate in at home?

In employment outside the home for fitness?

In employment outside the home for sociability?

In employment outside the home for entertainment?

In employment did you have membership in clubs and associations?

Describe your feelings when you lost your job?

In what ways did job loss affect your personal goals?

After job loss were your relationships with the family affected?

After unemployment, participation in the home?

After unemployment, participation outside the home for fitness?

After unemployment, participation outside the home for sociability?

After unemployment, participation outside the home for entertainment?

After unemployment, participation in clubs and associations?

What attempts have you made to get another job?

What personal resources do you have?

What external supports have you used?

APPENDIX C
In Depth Interview Schedule with Unemployed People

When you first lost your job, can you describe to me the psychological state you were in?

How do you feel about being out of work?

Between the time you lost your job and now? Has your condition changed?

What steps have you taken to find work?

What are the frustration's you faced in getting a job?

Do you seek work as keenly as when you first lost your job?

How do you cope with reduced income?

What are the kinds of things you did when you were employed and you can't do when you are unemployed?

What effect did job loss have on the activities in the home?

Do you visit your family often?

What effect did job loss have on the activities in the home?

What effect did job loss have on out-of-home activities?

What inner resources and skills do you have to cope with life without work?

What external resources and skills do you use to cope with life without work?

Do you have new interests and joined new organisations?

Besides financial loss, what effects has job loss had on your life?

APPENDIX D
Interview with Providers of Leisure Services

What is the philosophy of your organisation in regard to the provision and delivery of leisure services?

Is the philosophy of the organisation congruent with your personal views? Are there any differences, can you elaborate?

Have changes in the economic climate affected the strategies for the delivery of services?

Are your leisure services leased out to private contractors?

Are the objectives of the contractors consistent with those of your organisation?

Are concessions made for participation of disadvantaged segments of the community?

Do you feel that young people should be encouraged to lead healthy lifestyles?

Do you have any schemes in place to encourage greater participation of unemployed young people in activities that your organisation offers?

If you so not have schemes, would you be prepared to implement one? Would you get support from the organisation?

If you feel that programs should be provided for unemployed young people, how would you implement them, given that they have financial difficulties?

What measures would you take to identify unemployed young people in your local authority?

Would you be in favour of having specific programs of mainstream programs in which young people could participate?

Given unobligated tome your unemployed people have, would you take into account programming for them. Give some suggestions?

Do you have any ideas on how you can get unemployed young people involved in leisure programs under your control?

References

Alcock, P. (1997, 2nd ed.). *Understanding poverty.* London, Routledge.

Baker, J. (1993). *It's not Working: Unemployment in Australia.* Carlton, Vic.: CIS Publishers

Brenner, S. and S. Leui, L. (1987). Long-term unemployment among women in Sweden, *Social Science and Medicine*, 25(2), pp. 152-161.

Brewer, G. (1980). Out of work, out of sight: A study of the impact of unemployment on a group of Australian people. Melbourne: Brotherhood of St. Laurence.

Brownlee, I. (ed.) (1992). *Basic documents on human rights.* Oxford: Clarendon Press.

Cass, B. (1988). *Income support for the unemployed in Australia: Towards a more active system.* Canberra: Social Security Review: Issues Paper 4., Australian Government Printing Service.

Collins, M.F. and Kennett, C. (1998). Including poor people in leisure services without stigma: Leisure cards in the UK. *World Leisure and Recreation.* 40 (4), 17-22.

Crompton, J.L. (1987). Doing more with less in the delivery of parks and recreation services. State College, PA: Venture.

Crooks, M.L. (1996). *The price we pay: Young people poverty and long-term unemployment in Australia.* Hobart, Tasmania: National Clearing House for Youth Studies.

Durrance, G. and Hughes, H. (1996). *Working Youth – Tackling Australian Youth Unemployment.* Sydney: Centre for Independent Studies.

Eckersley, R. (1997). Portraits of Youth: Understanding young people's relationship with the future. *Futures,* Vol. 29, No. 3, pp. 243-249.

Edginton, C.R. & Compton, D.M. (1975). Consumerism and advocacy: A conceptual framework for the therapeutic recreator. *Therapeutic Recreation Journal,* 9(1), 271-29.

Edginton, C.R., Hanson, C.J., Edginton, S.R. & Hudson, S.D. (1998). *Leisure programming: A service-centred and benefits approach.* Boston, Massachusetts: WCB McGraw-Hill.

Evans, S.T. and Haworth, J.T. (1991). Variations in personal activity, access to categories of experience and psychological well-being in unemployed young adults, *Leisure Studies,* 10, 249-64.

Ezzy, D. (1993). Unemployment and mental health: A critical review. *Social Science and Medicine, 37, (1),* 41-52.

Fagin, M. and Little, M. (1984). *The forsaken families.* Harmondsworth: Penguin.

Frey, R., Reid, W. and Liekefett, L. (1995). Children, young people and unemployment. In R. Hicks, P. Creed, W. Patton and J. Tomlinson, Eds. *Unemployment Developments and Transitions.* (pp. 170-80), Brisbane: Australian Academic Press.

Fryer, D. (1995a). Social and psychological consequences of unemployment: From interviewing to intervening? In R. Hicks, P. Creed, W. Patton, and J. Tomlinson (Eds.), *Unemployment developments and transitions.* (pp. 58-76), Brisbane, Australian Academic Press.

Fryer, D. (1995b). Benefit Agency? Labour market disadvantage, deprivation and mental health, *The Psychologist,* 265-95.

Fryer, D.M. and Payne, R. (1984). Proactive behaviour in unemployment: findings and implications, *Leisure Studies,* 3, 273-95.

Fryer, D.M. and Payne, R. (1986). Being unemployed: A review of the literature on the psychological experience of unemployment. In C. L. Cooper and I. Robertson (Eds.), *International review of industrial and organisational psychology.* (pp. 235-278). Chichester, Wiley.

Fryer, D. M., and Warr, P.B. (1984). Unemployment and cognitive difficulties. *British Journal of Clinical Psychology, 23*, 67-68.

Gallic, D., Gershuny, J. and Vogler, C. (1995). Unemployment, the household and social networks. In D. Gallie, C. Marsh and C. Vogler (eds.) *Social change and the experience of unemployment..* (pp. 231-263). Oxford: Oxford University Press.

Glaser, B. and Strauss, A. (1971). *The discovery of grounded theory.* Chicago: Aldine

Glyptis, S. (1989). *Leisure and unemployment.* Milton Keynes: Open University Press.

Glyptis, S. (1994). Leisure provision for the unemployed: imperative or irrelevant? *World Leisure and Recreation, 36*(4), 34-39.

Goffman, E. (1968). Stigma: Notes on the management of spoiled identity. Harmondsworth: Penguin.

Guérin, C. (1984). Insertion professionelle difficile et socialisation des jeunes: Les jeunes chômeurs on-ils des loisirs? ADRAC. Actes du Congrès Mondial de Recherche sur le Temps Libre et le Loisir, Mary-le-Roi, 24-28, September 1984, 111, 5, 16-20.

Hammarstom, R. (1994). Health consequences of youth unemployment: Review from a gender perspective. *Social Science and Medicine,* 38(5), pp. 699-709.

Howard, D.R. & Crompton J.L. (1980). Financing, managing, and marketing recreation and park resources. Dubuque, IA: Wm. C. Brown.

Haworth, J.T. (1997a) *Work Leisure and Well-being,* London, Routledge.

Haworth, J.T. (1997b). Variations in lifestyle, access to categories of experience and well-being in young unemployed people. *World Leisure and Recreation.* 39(4), 14-17.

Haworth, J.T. and Ducker, J. (1991). Psychological well-being and access to categories of experience in unemployed young adults, *Leisure Studies,* 10, 265-74.

Haworth, J.T. and Evans, S.T. (1987). Meaningful activity and unemployment. In D. Fryer and P. Ullah (Eds.), *Unemployed people: Social and psychological perspectives.* (pp. 241-267). Milton Keynes: Open University Press.

Hayes, J. & Nutman, P. (1981). Understanding the unemployed: The psychological effects of unemployment. London: Tavistock Publications.

Heathwood, G. (1992). *Back on top, Finding yourself, Finding a job*. North Sydney: Allen and Unwin.

Hedges, A. (1985). Group interviewing. In A. Walker (Ed.), *Applied qualitative research*. (pp. 71-91). Vermont: Gower Publishing.

Henderson, K.A. (1991). *Dimensions of Choic*. State College PA: Venture Publishing, Inc.

Hepworth, S.J. (1980). Moderating factors of psychological impact of unemployment. *Journal of Occupational Psychology, 53*, 139-146.

Hill, J. (1977). The social and psychological impact of unemployment: A pilot study. *Tavistock Institute of Human Relations No. 2T*: 74.

ILAM (1997). Best Value: a definition and process, fact sheet 97/10. Goring upon Thames: ILAM.

Jahoda, M. (1979). The impact of unemployment in the 1930s and 1970s, *Bulletin of the British Psychological Society, 32*, 309-314.

Jahoda, M. (1981). Work, employment and unemployment: Values, theories and approaches in social research. *American Psychologist, 36*, 184-191.

Jahoda, M. (1984). Social institutions and human needs: a comment on Fryer and Payne, *Leisure Studies, 3*, 297-299.

Jahoda, M. (1986). In defence of non-reductionist social psychology, *Social Behaviour*, 25-29.

Jahoda, M. (1992). Reflections on Marienthal and after, *Journal of Occupational and Organisational Psychology, 65*, 355-358.

Kay, T. (1990). Active unemployment: A leisure pattern for the future? *Loisir et Societe, 12*, 413-430.

Kay, T. (1994). When great expectations reach their journeys end: accepting the limits of leisure provision of the unemployed, *World Leisure and Recreation, 36*(4), 29-33.

Kay, T. (1997). Researching women, unemployment and leisure. *Newsletter*, RC13 of the International Sociological Association, September, 1997.

Kelly, G. (1980). A study of the manager's orientation towards the transition from work to retirement. Unpublished PhD thesis, University of Leeds, UK.

Kelly, J.R. (1997). Activity and ageing: challenge in retirement. Guest chapter in J.T. Haworth, *Work, Leisure and Well-being*, London, Routledge, pp. 165-179.

Kevin, P., Dewberry, C., and Morley-Bunker, N. (1984). *Unemployment and leisure.* Report of the Sports Council/Economic and Social Research Council Joint Panel on Leisure and Recreation Research: London.

Kelvin, P. and Jarrett, J.E. (1985). *Unemployment: Its social psychological effects.* Cambridge: Cambridge University Press.

Kilpatrick R. and Trew, K. (1985). Lifestyles and psychological well-being among unemployed men in Northern Ireland. *Journal of Occupational Psychology.* 58, 207-216.

Kraus, R. (1997). *Recreation in modern society.* (5th ed.). Menlo Park: Benjamin Cummings.

Langmore, J. and Quiggin, J. (1994). *Work for all: Full employment in the nineties.* Carlton: Melbourne University Press.

Leana, C.R. and Feldman, D.C. (1995). Finding a new job after a plant closing: Antecedents and outcomes of the occurrence and quality of reemployment. *Human Relations*, 48, 1381-1401.

Lobo, F. (1994). *Late career unemployment: Its impact on lifestyle.* Unpublished PhD thesis. Perth: University of Western Australia.

Lobo, F. (1996). The effects of late career unemployment on lifestyle, *Loisir et Société*, 19(1) 167-194.

Lobo, F. (1997). Young people, leisure and unemployment in Western Australia. *World Leisure and Recreation.* 39(4), 4-9.

Lobo, F. (1998). The impact of unemployment on leisure: three variations. *Australian Parks and Leisure.* December, (34), 4.

Lobo, F. (1999). Young people and unemployment: Does job loss diminish involvement in leisure? *Loisir et Société / Society and Leisure* 22(1) 145-170.

Lobo, F. (1999a). The provision of sport and recreation for unemployed young adults. Study prepared for Healthway, Western Australian Health Promotion Foundation, Edith Cowan University, Perth, Western Australia.

Lobo, F. (2000). Youth unemployment: impediment or catalyst to leisure and human development. Paper presented at the 6th World Leisure Congress, University of Deusto, Bilbao, Spain, July 3-7.

Lobo, F. and Parker, S. (1999). *Late Career Unemployment: Impacts on Self, Family and Lifestyles.* Williamstown, Victoria: HM Leisure Planning Pty. Ltd.

Lobo, F. & Watkins, G. (1995). Late career unemployment in the 1990s: It impact on the family. *Journal of Family Studies.* 1(2), 103-113.

Lynn, R., Hampson, S. and Magee, M. (1984). Home background, intelligence, personality and education as predictors of unemployment in young people. *Personal and Individual Differences,* 5, 549-557.

MacDonald, H. (1997). Assisting young unemployed people: Directions for employment assistance programs. *World Leisure and Recreation.* 39(4). 27-30.

Meyer, H.D. & Brightbill, C.K. (1948). *Recreation administration: A guide to its practices.* Englewood Cliffs, New Jersey: Prentice-Hall.

Morris, L. (1994). Dangerous classes: the underclass and social citizenship. London: Routledge.

Murphy, J.F. (1980). An enabling approach to leisure delivery. In T.L. Goodale and P.A. Witt, (Eds.), *Recreation and leisure: Issues in an era of change,* pp. 197-210, State College, PA: Venture.

National Council for the International Year of the Family. (1994). *Creating links: Families and social responsibility.* Canberra: Australian Government Publishing Service.

National Recreation Participation Survey. (1991). Analysed by the Centre of Leisure and Tourism, cited by Lynch, R. and Veal A.J. (1996) *Australian Leisure,* Sydney: Longman, p. 128.

National Statistics Office (1998). *GHS 1996.* London, HMSO.

Nichols, G. (1997). The role of sports counselling for unemployed young people on probation. *World Leisure and Recreation.* 39(4).

Niepoth, W.F. (1983). *Leisure leadership.* Englewood Cliffs, NJ. Prentice-Hall.

Parker, S. (1999). Socialist views and experiences. *Leisure Issues,* 2(2) pp.2-3.

Patton, M.Q. (1987). *How to use qualitative methods in evaluation.* London: Sage Publications.

Payne, R.L., Warr, P.B., and Hartley, J. (1984). Social class and psychological ill-health during employment. *Sociology of Health and Illness,* 6, 152-174.

Pusey, M. (1991). *Economic rationalism in Canberra.* Cambridge: Cambridge University Press.

Rapoport, R. (1982). Unemployment and the family. The Loch Memorial Lecture 1981, The Family Welfare Association, London.

Richards, L. (1992). *NUDIST. (Computer program) Version 2.3.* Melbourne: La Trobe University.

Roberts, K. (1992). Leisure theories in the field of youth. Congrès Mondial Loisirs et Jeunesse, INJEP, Marly-le-Roi, 17-20 November 1992.

Roberts, K. (1997). Work and leisure in young peoples lives. Guest chapter in J.T. Haworth, *Work, Leisure and Well-Being,* London, Routledge, pp. 143-164.

Roberts, K. (1999). Do we know what leisure is good for people? *Leisure Issues,* 2(1), p. 2.

Roberts, K., Brodie, D. & Dench, S. (1987). Youth unemployment and out-of-home recreation. *Leisure Studies, (10)* 2, 281-294.

Robinson, L. (2000). Following the quality strategy: the reasons for the use of quality management in UK public leisure facilities. *Leisure Studies Association Newsletter,* No. 55, March, pp. 26-36.

Roche, J. (1997). Children's rights: participation and dialogue. In J. Roche and S. Tucker (Eds.). *Youth in Society.* 49-58. London: Sage and The Open University.

Room, G., with Sada, G.A., Benington, J., Breda, J., Giannichedda, M.G., Guillen, E., Henningsen, B., Laezko, F., Madiera, J., Mylonakis, D., O'Cinneide, S., Robbins, D., Whitting, G. (1993). *Anti-poverty research in Europe,* Briston: SAUS.

Rushkoff, D. (1996). Playing the future: How kids' culture can teach us to thrive in an age of chaos. London: Harper Collins.

Sader, E. (1998). Work, unemployment and spare time. Paper presented at the *5th World Congress of the World Leisure and Recreation Association,* Sao Paulo, Brazil.

Siegal, S. and Castellan Jr., N.J. (1988). *Non parametric statistics for the behavioural sciences,* (2nd Edition), New York: McGraw Hill International Series.

Siegal, R.L., (1994). *Employment and Human Rights.* Philadelphia: University of Pennsylvania.

Storer, M. (1998). Thank for nothing. In K. Healey (Ed.), Unemployment in Australia, *Issues in Society,* Vol. 96. Balmain, NSW: The Spinney Press.

Swinburne, P. (1981). The psychological impact of unemployment on managers and professional staff. *Journal of Occupational Psychology*, 54, 47-64.

Tiggeman, M. and Winefield, A.H. (1989). Predictors of employment, unemployment and further study among school-leavers. *Journal of Occupational Psychology*, 62, 213-221.

Torkildsen, G. (1992). *Leisure and recreation management.* London: E&FN Spon.

Townsend, P. (1979). Poverty in the UK: A survey of household resources and standards of living. London: Penquin.

Wanberg, C., Watt, J.D. and Rumsey, D.J. (1996). Individuals without jobs: An empirical study of job-seeking behaviour and reemployment. *Journal of Applied Psychology, 81,* 76-87.

Warr, P.B. and Jackson, P. (1984). Men without jobs: Some correlates of age and length of employment. *Journal of Occupational Psychology, 57,* 77-85.

Watts, M. (2000). The dimensions and costs of unemployment in Australia. In S. Bell (Ed.) *The Unemployment Crisis in Australia.* Cambridge: Cambridge University Press.

Williams, C. (2000). Monitoring of public sector leisure services by best value. *Leisure Studies Association Newsletter*, No. 55, March, pp. 37-40.

World Leisure (1998). Sao Paulo Declaration. Adopted October 30, 1998 in Sao Paulo, Brazil, at the 5th *World Congress of the World Leisure and Recreation Association* (WLRA), held in conjunction with Servico Do Comérico (SESC), Sao Paulo, and the Latin America Leisure and Recreation Association (ALATIR). Author. 12(2), 3-4.

Index